Ephesians and Colossians Diagrammed in Greek

Ephesians and Colossians Diagrammed in Greek

Randy A. Leedy

GLOSSAHOUSE
WILMORE, KY
WWW.GLOSSAHOUSE.COM

Ephesians and Colossians Digrammed in Greek by Randy A. Leedy

Diagrams and notes, originally in digital form: © 2005, 2012, 2020 BibleWorks LLC, jointly with Randy A. Leedy, 2020

Diagrams and notes, print edition: © 2021 GlossaHouse

All rights reserved. No part of this work may be reproduced or transmitted in any form or by any means, electronic or mechanical, including photocopying and recording, or by means of any information storage or retrieval system, except as may be expressly permitted by the 1976 Copyright Act or in writing from the publisher. Requests for permission should be addressed in writing to:

GlossaHouse, LLC
110 Callis Circle
Wilmore, KY 40390

ISBN: 978-1-63663-0328 (pb)

Library of Congress Control Number: 2022918937

Cover design by T. Michael W. Halcomb.

Greek New Testament Text: Nestle-Aland, Novum Testamentum Graece, 28th Revised Edition, edited by Barbara and Kurt Aland, Johannes Karavidopoulos, Carlo M. Martini, and Bruce M. Metzger in cooperation with the Institute for New Testament Textual Research, Münster/Westphalia, © 2012 Deutsche Bibelgesellschaft, Stuttgart. Used by permission.

Dedication

This print edition of these diagrams is dedicated to
Dr. Samuel E. Schnaiter,
Longtime chairman of the Greek Department of
Bob Jones University.

You taught me and so many others
to love the Greek New Testament
and to exert ourselves to the utmost
to discern the meaning of its every detail.
And you led us in having fun as we did it!

οὐ ἄδικος ὁ θεὸς
ἐπιλαθέσθαι τοῦ ἔργου ὑμῶν καὶ τῆς ἀγάπης
ἧς ἐνεδείξασθε εἰς τὸ ὄνομα αὐτοῦ.
Hebrews 6:10

Henceforth there is laid up for you, too,
a crown of righteousness,
which the Lord, the righteous judge,
shall give you at that day.
2 Timothy 4:8

Contents

Preface 1

Introduction 3

Ephesians Diagrams 17

Colossians Diagrams 49

New Testament Greek Sentence Diagramming 74

Diagramming Policies 100

Preface

This is a sample of a planned multi-volume print edition of the Greek New Testament Sentence Diagrams as published in BibleWorks software. A few features and characteristics of the work deserve explanation.

The diagrams were drawn within the diagramming environment provided in BibleWorks software, now out of business. A proprietary document format uniquely developed for BibleWorks makes the diagrams essentially uneditable in any other software environment. This fact, combined with a need for cost efficiency in the production of a print edition, requires maintaining the pagination of the BibleWorks presentation of the diagrams. A desire to minimize page breaks within diagrams combines with this fact to produce what may at first glance appear to be an excessive amount of white space on many pages. Since these diagrams will undoubtedly elicit, for many users, a desire to make notes and sketch alternative constructions, that white space may well prove to be a feature rather than a drawback.

A page-layout challenge arises from the fact that the work includes over 1,000 annotations to the diagrams. In what form should these annotations appear? The obvious possibilities that leap to mind are to place each note as close as possible to the text that it deals with, or to place at the end of each chapter all the notes pertaining to that chapter, or to place each book's notes at the end of the book, or to place all notes pertaining to a volume of the diagrams in an appendix at the end of that volume, or, finally, to publish the notes in an entirely separate volume.

Each of these options, in sequence, is progressively more troublesome to the user but, with the exception of the last, more advantageous to the publisher. In this sample volume, we have chosen the second option and have placed all the notes for each chapter in a group at the end of the chapter. A shaded dagger symbol at the right margin of a page of diagrams alerts the reader to the presence of a note on a portion of the diagram at that approximate vertical position on the page. Each note begins with a verse reference to assist the reader in finding the note corresponding to each dagger.

PREFACE

We have included interior verse references for diagrams spanning more than a single verse. Since extensive sentence diagrams never preserve the word order of the text, segmentation of a diagram by verse breaks can never by crystal clear. We hope, though, that the addition of these references will provide enough help to be worth the space on the page and the production time required to add them.

A final observation is that the BibleWorks diagramming environment, not being designed to support professional-quality print production, places unfortunate limits on the print quality that this production could achieve. To redo all the diagrams from scratch in a professional graphics environment is cost-prohibitive. We hope that the print quality will be at least marginally acceptable to all readers and that the value of the diagrams, made available as economically as possible, will justify the unavoidable shortcoming.

Introduction

Documentation Package Overview

The documentation provided for the New Testament Greek Sentence Diagrams consists of three parts. The first—this one—presents basic orientation to the diagrams and the supporting documentation. The second, provided as an appendix, is a primer on Greek sentence diagramming written for *Biblical Viewpoint* (the former journal of the School of Religion of Bob Jones University). The third, a further appendix, presents in detail the policies developed and followed in the preparation of these diagrams.

I beg the reader's indulgence regarding my extensive use of the passive voice and especially of the first person, in violation of ordinary conventions of academic writing. My intention in this document is not to legislate a set of policies that must be followed in Greek sentence diagramming but rather to describe what I actually do in my own diagramming and what I did in these diagrams in particular. I make no claim that mine is the only way, but I want the user of the diagrams to have available a fairly full description of what I did and why. Legislation could easily be written in the third person, active voice, but non-binding description of one's own practices cannot. Please do not construe the use of the first person as egocentric, then, but rather as implying the reader's liberty to deal with the matters under discussion otherwise than I have done.

About the Author

Assuming that I may continue to write in the first person, I identify myself as a native of Mansfield, Ohio, a graduate of Dalton High School (Dalton, Georgia, 1978) and Bob Jones University (Greenville, SC), where I earned the B.A. in Bible in 1982, M.A. in Bible in 1984, and Ph.D. in New Testament Interpretation in 1991. Beginning in 1982 I served at Bob Jones University as a Graduate Assistant teaching Greek, a supervisor in the J. S. Mack Library, a Bible curriculum writer for the Bob Jones University Press, and, from 1994 until 2019, as Professor of New Testament in the Bob Jones University Seminary. I have also been privileged to serve local churches in the roles of Sunday School teacher, visitation director,

INTRODUCTION

elder, assistant pastor, and pastor. I am married to the former Katie Rymer, of Westerville, Ohio, and God has blessed us with three children (Diana, Benjamin, and Daniel), three children in-law, and, so far, five grandchildren.

Since it is not possible to do the kind of work represented by these diagrams from a presuppositional vacuum, I wish to inform the reader of the theological persuasion with which I approach my work. I understand that many users of the diagrams will not share this persuasion, and the discussions included in this document do not engage in arm-twisting. Those who disagree with me will nevertheless want to know where I stand so that they may take that stance into account as they use this work.

I locate myself firmly within the Fundamentalist branch of Protestant Christianity, intending *Fundamentalist* in its classic sense when the word was coined in the early 1900s—a sense that, unfortunately, has suffered significant corruption in more recent times by its use as a descriptor for a variety of extremist movements. Based on the Bible's statement about itself, I believe that the sixty-six canonical books of scripture are God's authoritative Word, given originally by a miraculous and unexplainable process by which God spoke through the human authors in such a way that their words are His words, completely infallible and inerrant in every particular, though subject to misunderstanding and imperfect transmission resulting from the fallibility of those who have handled them subsequently to the original writing, whom God did not see fit to continue to protect from all error by an ongoing miracle.

In the reading and study of those books I subscribe to the grammatical-historical school of interpretation, and I believe that God has equipped humanity with capacities allowing the careful, honest reader to discern the author's original intention with an accuracy sufficient to allow him to grasp all necessary details of the intended message. Thus these sentence diagrams are not an exercise in laying out "what this passage communicates to me" but rather "what the author's words indicate that he intended." Of course I am not able to eliminate my own subjectivity as an interpreter; I cannot find that God has provided any means by which I can succeed in doing so. But I am constantly doing my best to find the most objective possible bases on which to choose among the various options for construing the grammar. It is a subtle but important difference whether one is looking for the understanding that most pleases him or for that which commends itself as most likely what the author intended. The latter is my goal,

INTRODUCTION

though I am certain that even my best efforts have fallen short of complete success. However, I am aware of no better goal toward which to strive than that of discovering the author's original intent, nor am I aware of any approach better suited to achieve that goal than the presuppositions and methods reflected in the work presented here.

History of the Diagrams

As might be expected, the history of these sentence diagrams is somewhat complex. The early years of my teaching career (mid-1980s) coincided with developments in computer technology that were exciting for students of the original languages of scripture. Using the early font editor program for the Macintosh, a colleague of mine devised a Hebrew font and I devised a Greek font that were used by many at Bob Jones University for a number of years. In the late 1980s I switched from the Mac to the PC in order to use GRAMCORD (www.Gramcord.org) for my doctoral dissertation. From descriptions I had read, I was hoping that GRAMCORD would allow me to perform searches in which syntactical connections (such as subject-verb) could serve as search criteria. I was disappointed to find that the only search criteria available were those related to forms, lemmas, parsing details, and word order. I ended up having to create my own database of syntactical connections (limited to those I had singled out for study) for the epistle to the Hebrews, which was the focus of my dissertation work.

A few years passed between the completion of my dissertation and my beginning to teach Seminary-level Greek, during which time Logos Bible Software and BibleWorks had come onto the scene. Advertisements made it clear that I needed to acquire one of these programs, but the prices prohibited the acquisition of both. After some weeks of praying for some form of guidance about which one I should purchase, I woke up one morning with a thought: I could get review copies of both programs in order to write a significant article comparing the two for *Biblical Viewpoint*, which at that time was the journal of Bob Jones University's School of Religion and Seminary. The plan worked to perfection, and I was able to get both programs free of charge, learn their capabilities, and then offer the public the fruit of my comparison. An electronic version of that review received fairly wide distribution in the middle and later 1990s.

INTRODUCTION

Anyone who has worked with complex software in any depth at all has experienced the reality that some functions do not work, some work incorrectly, and some functions that would be helpful are not provided. And where there is data, there are errors! So in the process of developing that review, I ended up in rather extensive correspondence with both Logos and BibleWorks. In the course of that correspondence, I voiced my desire for what I had always wanted: a searchable syntax database of the Greek New Testament. I knew that a perfect database was unattainable (since syntax is subject to ambiguity and individual interpretation), but I hoped that something could come into existence that would prove much better than nothing.

When BibleWorks added a sentence diagramming environment (in version 4 or 5, as I recall), it seemed natural to them to follow up with the development of a set of sentence diagrams for the whole Greek New Testament. Mike Bushell, owner of the company, asked me whether I was interested in the project. I had never diagrammed seriously, but the plan was exciting to me: the diagramming symbols would have metadata attached that would allow the eventual development of a search engine that could locate grammatical constructions independently of the Greek words involved or their order in the sentence.

When a sabbatical from teaching proved untenable, I undertook the project on a part-time basis beginning in the summer of 2004 and extending through the end of the summer of 2006. Over that period of two school years and three summers, I spent about 2,000 hours preparing about 2,000 pages of diagrams and associated annotations, which numbered a little over 1,000. BibleWorks published this work in stages, beginning with the Pauline Epistles. Upon its completion, the package was peer-reviewed by Rodney Decker (now with the Lord but whose website www.NTResources.com continues to be helpful to many) and received his strong approval.

The search engine for the diagrams still awaits development. Personnel of the former BibleWorks have expressed some optimism that these files would prove decipherable to an experienced programmer, for the extraction of syntactical metadata. Anyone wishing to pursue possible development of a search engine is welcome to contact me for discussion.

Since the release of the diagrams in BibleWorks, a significant number of corrections to both diagrams and notes have been made, but no large-scale revision. I continue to notice errors, but only rarely, and I receive little corrective input from users.

Upon the publication of Nestle-Aland's 28th edition, the diagrams were revised from their original NA27 text to implement the textual changes made in the new edition, which were limited to the General Epistles. I also ran an electronic document comparison of the 27th and 28th editions in search of any changes in punctuation or capitalization that might affect the diagrams or notes and implemented the very few revisions required.

In the Fall of 2020, I made moderately extensive revisions to incorporate various kinds of tweaks, to expand the grammatical notes somewhat, and to correct some rather embarrassingly serious errors. At this point I envision no large-scale future revisions to the NA28 version, though I do not absolutely rule out that possibility.

Orientation to the Diagrams

Preliminary Discussions

The first objection that came to mind when I began to contemplate drawing sentence diagrams for the whole Greek NT was that it seemed perhaps unwise to offer the public a work that could easily give the appearance of claiming to say the last word on matters of the basic syntax of the sentences of the Greek NT. Would users of the diagrams attach more authority to them than is warranted? Or would they wonder whether perhaps I were claiming unwarranted authority for them myself? I was able to put that concern to rest when I realized that every prospective commentator faces the same concern, and every student of scripture is thankful that the commentators have ventured forth in spite of such misgivings. The commentator has the advantage of communicating in a form that makes it easy for him to express his uncertainties and reservations, but he would be a tedious commentator who did so constantly. A writer must be able to express his understanding simply, with an expectation that the reader will understand that he claims no Sinaitic authority for his claims.

So let it be understood from the outset that these diagrams are offered as nothing more (or less!) than the fruit of one man's wrestling with the syntax of the

INTRODUCTION

Greek NT from the vantage point of some experience in its study and teaching. Further, though they have existed for almost fifteen years now, they remain in essentially their first draft, having received only limited correction. Only time will tell to what extent they will eventually be revised, whether by me or by others. One thing is certain: the diagrams are imperfect, and despite the efforts that have been invested in accuracy, there no doubt remain outright errors needing correction and weaknesses needing strengthened. With the conviction that one ought not to let his inability to say something he considers definitive muzzle him from saying something he considers legitimate, I have sent this work forth in hope that it will prove adequate and may perhaps even find a lasting place among the reference sources valued by students of the Greek New Testament.

Whether the work will prove to have any lasting value depends in part upon the fate of traditional approaches to grammar among Biblical exegetes of the future. Current thought is raising rather serious questions about the validity of traditional grammar. While I think it is highly likely that grammarians may often have fancied their systems more definitive than they actually are, it is not at all clear to me that newer approaches that dismiss a great deal of traditional grammar will produce overall improvement in the process by which language is analyzed for the sake of discerning meaning.

Better, it seems to me, is to recognize that language simply does not submit itself to as rigid a classification scheme as careful students might wish, and to retain what appears to be a valid core of traditional grammatical understanding while loosening up around the edges for more flexibility than previous generations of students may have recognized. It is hard for me to imagine that analysis along the lines of "this noun is the subject of this verb" or "this adverb modifies this infinitive" will ever become outmoded. Unfashionable, I can well imagine, but I doubt that it will superseded by some completely different approach that will yield more objectively verifiable exegetical fruit. If it does, traditionally drawn diagrams like these will deserve their ensuing death, and the wise will not lament their passing. It will be enough if such diagrams have served their own generation by the will of God (cf. Acts 13:36).

So, although the relatively recent resurgence in traditional sentence diagramming as an exegetical exercise has met with disrespect in some quarters, those who have combined to produce these diagrams make no apology for this kind of work, believing that it reflects the soundest approach to the syntactical aspect of

INTRODUCTION

grammatical-historical interpretation currently known. The fact that a map of Yosemite National Park, for example, is a poor substitute for an actual visit to the park does not undermine the value of the map for its appropriate purposes. Would be we be better off today if all prospective cartographers in past generations had decided to draw no maps for fear that their work might prove imperfect or inadequate? Certainly traditional diagramming can be faulted at numerous points. But until a superior alternative for mapping out human speech arises and proves itself, let us continue to value traditional diagramming for its merits while recognizing its defects to the extent that we are aware of them and correcting them to the extent that we are able.

A note of caution against excessively simplistic use of the diagrams is warranted. Everyone realizes that recent decades have seen an explosion of the quantity of information accessible to the average person, mostly by electronic means. It is easy to mistake the availability of information for the solution to a problem. In the medical realm, for example, one may be able to find information about personal health issues. But seeing words and pictures about solving medical problems is obviously not at all the same as being healthy. Most, of course, are not especially interested in the information for its own sake; what they really want is health. The information is a means to the end, not the end itself. Similarly, a Bible student who pursues the exegesis of the Biblical text in the original or modern languages has an interest in the lexicography and grammar of those languages, not as ends in themselves but as means to the end of confidence about the valid meaning or meanings of the text. When we understand that information is a means and not an end, we are in a position to see clearly that no less critical to a successful outcome than the suitability of the means is the skill with which the various means are employed. The most accurate information and the most expensive medical instrumentation are of no use—indeed they may prove damaging—to a practitioner unable to use those means properly.

Let us consider another illustration that provides a closer parallel to sentence diagramming. Imagine a television breaking down in the year 1960, when such items were usually repaired rather than discarded. When the owner takes the TV to a repair shop, he assumes that the technician will have not one but two major things that he, the owner, lacks: not only *information* but also *understanding* about how the TV is supposed to work. The fact, however, that the average person now has access to most of the information that experts in any field rely upon does not constitute ordinary people experts in any field, regardless of how some

INTRODUCTION

may fancy themselves so. Information may be at our fingertips, but understanding remains an expensive and often elusive commodity. Online access to technical service manuals and schematic diagrams for a malfunctioning device will not allow an unskilled person to succeed in repairing it.

A repairman, of course, has an objective criterion by which to measure success: is he able to return the device to operational condition? If so, he has found a valid (though not necessarily the best) solution to the problem; if not, he must admit failure. But the case of the Bible student is different: the criteria by which to measure success in discovering valid meaning are not so simple or objective. For any given text he or she may formulate a meaning that is personally acceptable, producing a feeling of success. But is one's own satisfaction an adequate gauge of validity in interpretation? If that interpreter were then to consult half a dozen commentaries on the passage, all of whom agreed on a different meaning, would he or she remain satisfied with that initial understanding? Surely it would not be commendable "workmanship" for the interpreter in such a case to maintain his or her own interpretation on no surer basis than that it is personally satisfying.

At this point our discussion teeters on the brink of the seemingly bottomless chasm of Hermeneutics. So suffice it to warn that owning a set of sentence diagrams for the whole Greek New Testament does not equate to having access to the correct meaning of every New Testament sentence! Looking at a sentence diagram no more guarantees a correct solution to an interpretative problem than looking at a schematic diagram guarantees a correct solution to an electronic problem. Just as a schematic diagram is of great value to a trained repair technician, a sentence diagram can be of great value to a trained exegete looking for confirmation or correction of his current understanding or to a promising student looking to enlarge his or her mastery of the syntax of the Greek New Testament. The value of the diagrams for any user will correspond to the extent of that user's understanding of the grammatical matters which the diagrams map out.

As the author of the diagrams, I feel little anxiety over those who will find them opaque and dismiss them with the "Greek to me!" retort. They are none the worse for their attempt. The anxiety I feel is over any who may unskillfully use the diagrams to formulate misunderstandings of various texts, gaining misguided confidence that they have unlocked correct meaning from the Greek text when

INTRODUCTION

in fact they have done nothing of the sort. The owner of a web site posting instructions for surgical procedures without clear disclaimers warning against misuse of the information by untrained persons would almost certainly be held legally liable for deaths resulting from home surgeries performed by those wanting the benefits of professional medical care without the associated costs. And we can be sure that the motivation behind labels that a few decades ago began to appear on electrical devices warning against do-it-yourself repair is legal protection, not altruism. Fortunately, misusers of Greek sentence diagrams are not likely to experience dire consequences. While systemic misinterpretation of God's Word can indeed cause or contribute to eternal death, it is highly unlikely that the use or non-use of Greek NT sentence diagrams will produce or prevent that condition. So by all means, I want to encourage, not discourage the use of the diagrams!

Lesser problems, however, can certainly result from even well-intentioned misinterpretation, and I hope that users of these diagrams will be wary of the tendency to attribute too much validity to interpretations that cross their minds while reading them. What you are thinking may not be at all what I intended my diagram to communicate, and what I intended may not be at all what the author of the text intended! So please accept a caution against assuming that any idea about the meaning of a Biblical passage formulated while looking at Greek or Hebrew words or at legitimate information about them must automatically be correct. The best criteria by which to evaluate an interpretation, outside the primary grammatical and historical data of scripture itself, remains the community of faithful interpreters available in the form of careful and accurate translations and commentaries, varied as they may be. I have gratefully depended on many of them (especially the translators) as I diagrammed. My conscious dependence has been great; my unconscious dependence has probably been much greater.

It is my hope and prayer that these diagrams will be of service especially to those well embarked on the journey toward mastery of the grammatical aspects of the exegesis of the Greek New Testament and that those who are not yet prepared to make proper use of them will find in them not a stumbling block but rather an impetus toward the studies necessary for commendable exegesis of scripture.

INTRODUCTION

References Used in Producing the Work

The grammatical understanding that is the backbone of the diagrams is the product of something over 25 years of personal study and teaching of NT Greek with an eye to grammatical detail, developed in substantial degree under the tutelage of my major Greek professor at Bob Jones University, Samuel Schnaiter (to whom the print edition of these diagrams is dedicated). Other teachers and writers who have contributed to that study are numerous and untraceable, though all the major reference sources are included.

One can diagram hardly a verse without encountering some expression that might be construed more than one way. In the vast majority of these cases I have simply diagrammed as consistently as possible according to my own understanding rather than extending the time and expense of the work by chases through the literature that often would have proven unfruitful anyway.

This is not to say, however, that I diagrammed entirely out of my own head. The key reference sources used in selecting among various options for construing the grammar are BDAG (*A Greek-English Lexicon of the New Testament and Other Early Christian Literature*, third edition [2000], by Bauer, Danker, Arndt, and Gingrich)[1] and the body of English versions. Readers who regularly consult the notes will also find frequent reference to A. T. Robertson's *Word Pictures in the Greek New Testament*. If this dependence upon a rather badly outdated reference work appears puzzling, please remember that I originally drew these diagrams for inclusion in the BibleWorks Bible software package, and Robertson's work was the best grammatical commentary for the whole New Testament available to every BibleWorks user. I used it heavily because, though dated it is still respected, and I wanted users to be able to retrace my steps as easily as possible.

BDAG is generally given priority; a very strong consensus of versions was required to overrule it. However, I did not rigidly follow a hierarchical scheme of dependence upon others. Here and there I ventured out on my own, and I occasionally I let my own inclinations determine whether I would follow BDAG or a particular group of versions. I believe it is true that in every case where I con-

---

[1] Competent Greek students who have used BDAG extensively are not surprised to see this lexicon mentioned as a source for a work on Greek syntax. One of the remarkable features of that lexicon is the amount of information it contains about the grammatical structures surrounding the usage of the individual words of the NT Greek vocabulary stock.

sciously diagrammed contrary to both BDAG and the versions, I included a note on what I had done and why.

I am aware of the existence of NT Greek sentence diagrams prepared by Gerhard Raske. Before beginning my own work, I perused his web site and reviewed the samples posted there. I commend him for his gargantuan labors and for the amount of data he has managed to pack into his diagrams. In the samples I reviewed, however, I found some places where I felt his diagrams did not accurately capture the nature of the Greek constructions. So I do not believe my diagrams represent a pointless duplication of labor. In order to avoid any accidental plagiarism, at no point in the process of producing these diagrams did I consult Raske's work in any way. In fact, the only other diagrams I consulted at all are those on Colossians drawn by John Grassmick, whose work and my use of it receive attention in the presentation of diagramming policies in the back matter of this publication. Further, since the initial publication of these diagrams in BibleWorks, Accordance Bible Software has also published a similar set, and William Ramey is currently in the process of doing the same. To the extent that I have examined these works, they appear well done; I will leave the judgment about comparative quality to others. Wise exegetes eagerly compare multiple versions and commentaries, and it is encouraging to see a variety of diagram packages now available for comparison as well.

Consistency and completeness

I have attempted to diagram consistently across the whole New Testament. Consistency, however, is *much* more easily named as a virtue than accomplished as a fact. For example, the indirect object has a separate diagramming symbol from an adverbial modifier. On what basis does one determine whether a given dative noun is an indirect object or an adverbial dative? The basic rule of thumb is obvious: transitive verbs take objects, direct and indirect. But occasionally the dative with a transitive verb seems clearly to express a person advantaged or disadvantaged by the action rather than someone indirectly acted upon. Take the example of the verb ποιέω. In Mark 5:19, Jesus instructs the former demoniac to tell his family what He had done for him (ὅσα ὁ κύριός σοι πεποίηκεν). While the adverbial idea of personal interest certainly fits the context, the indirect object construction works equally well (Jesus performed the action of doing directly upon the "things" [ὅσα] and indirectly upon the man) and therefore might be

INTRODUCTION

chosen on the basis that ποιέω is transitive. But come to Mark 6:12, where Herod made (ποιέω) a feast for his important men, who are expressed in the dative. In this context I cannot bring myself to see those men as being indirectly acted upon, so I feel compelled to diagram the dative on the adverb symbol. Luke 7:5 (τὴν συναγωγὴν αὐτὸς ᾠκοδόμησεν ἡμῖν) seems clearly to *require* an adverbial connection to a transitive verb, unless one wishes to be quite broad in his understanding of what an *object* is.

But once I have introduced the possibility of using the adverb rather than the indirect object for a transitive verb, on what basis will I decide which to use in any given case? And, for that matter, how do I determine reliably in every case whether or not a verb is transitive? Since absolute consistency is at best highly elusive and probably unattainable, I have simply tried to be as consistent as possible without greatly vexing myself over the matter. I have often revised earlier diagrams in light of criteria developed through the process of exposure to variety of usage over the course of the work. Undoubtedly some resolvable inconsistency remains, despite my best intentions and efforts, and I will be grateful for feedback that helps me identify and eliminate it in any future revisions of the work.

I often found it impossible to diagram every thought connection within a sentence. Must every pronoun be connected to its antecedent? How could that connection be made when, for example, Paul says διὰ τοῦτο, where τοῦτο refers to a whole paragraph of argumentation? Luke 4:23 exemplifies another kind of difficulty, where Jesus said that He knew the people wanted Him to do "here, in your home town," the things they had heard of His doing elsewhere. The two adverbial elements modify "do," but they also equate to one another: "here" refers to the same place as "in your home town." The phrase "in your home town" can be diagrammed as adverbial to "do" or as appositional to "here," but not both, at least not within ordinary diagramming conventions. In such cases I diagrammed what seemed to me to be the most important connection, which in this case I deemed to be the adverbial one.

Similarly, sometimes a negative adverb introduces a question and signals whether the expected answer is positive or negative. Theoretically the word could be divided into two parts, the negative introducing the sentence and the rest of the word modifying the verb. This approach might work with some words but how would it work, for example, with οὐδέποτε in Matthew 21:16? Surely δέποτε can-

INTRODUCTION

not be diagrammed as a Greek adverb! Should the word be divided into all three of its parts, in order to be able at least to work with real Greek words? Or should the introductory negative in this case be οὐδέ rather than οὐ? And even if there were an obviously valid way to parcel out the pieces, by diagramming the negative as introductory to the sentence we would still lose the fact that it does contribute to the meaning of the adverb; it does not solely signal the expected answer. So the sentence diagrams should not be expected to account for every traceable thought connection within the syntax.

EPHESIANS

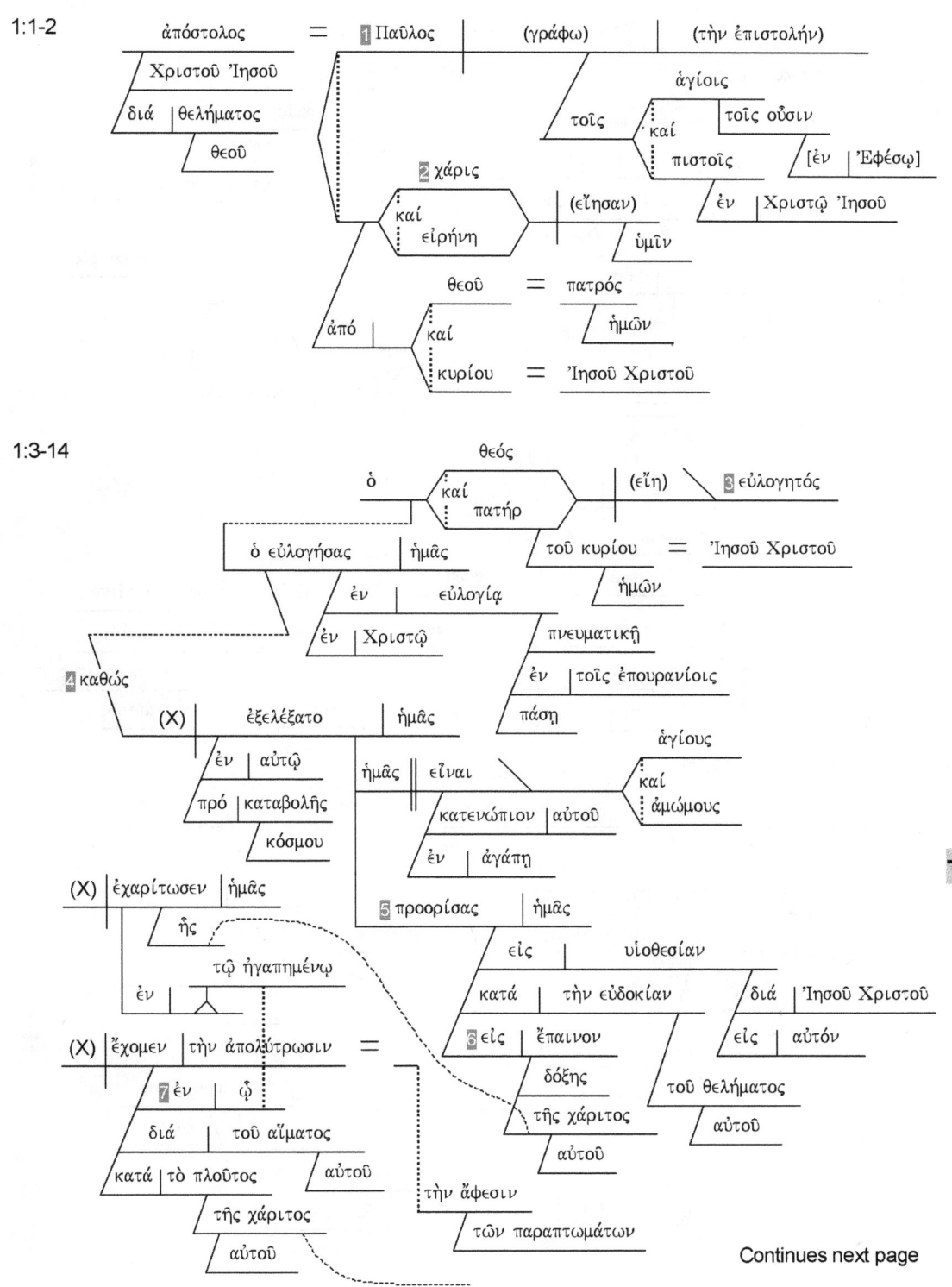

Continues next page

1:8-14 EPHESIANS

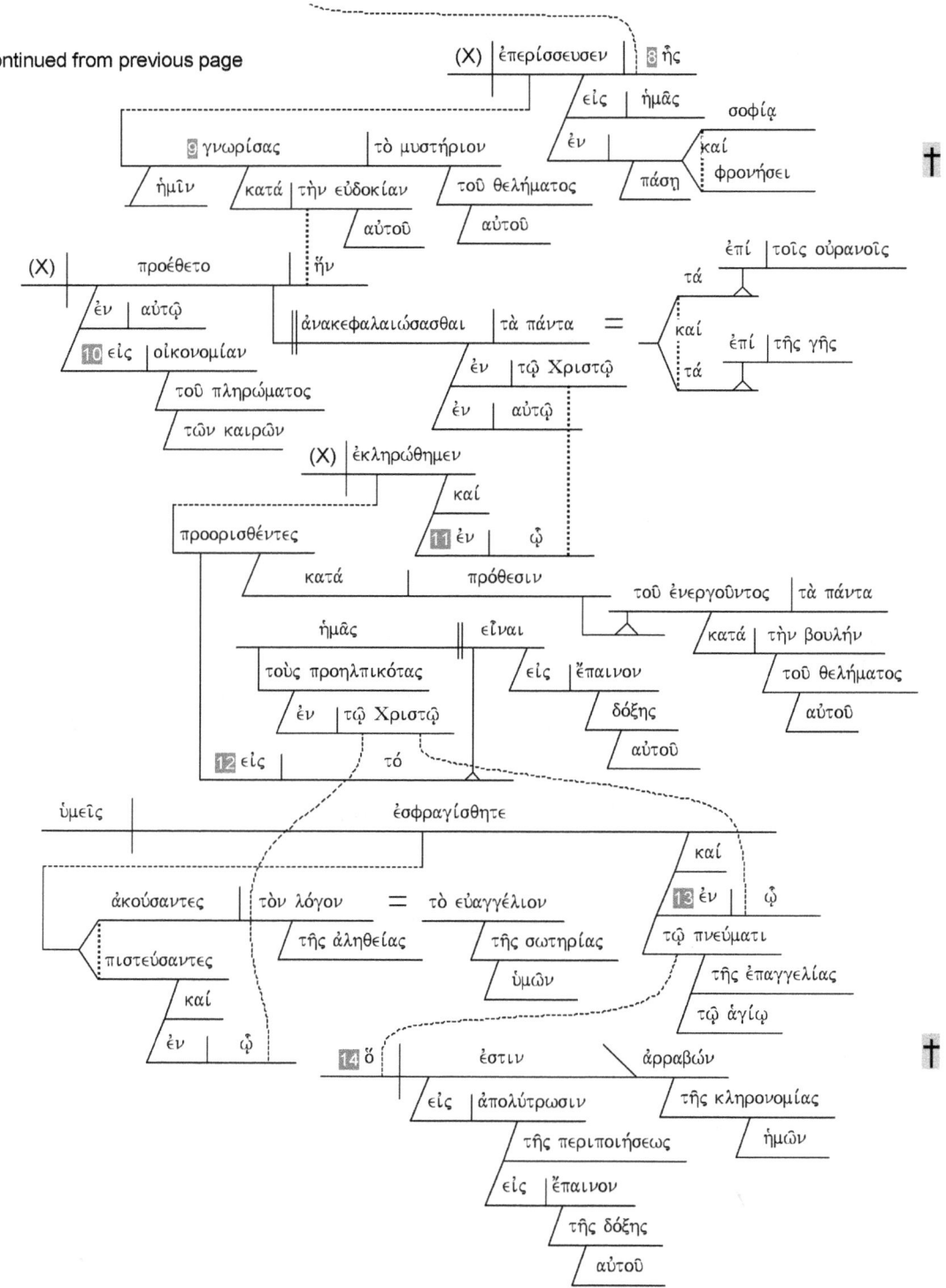

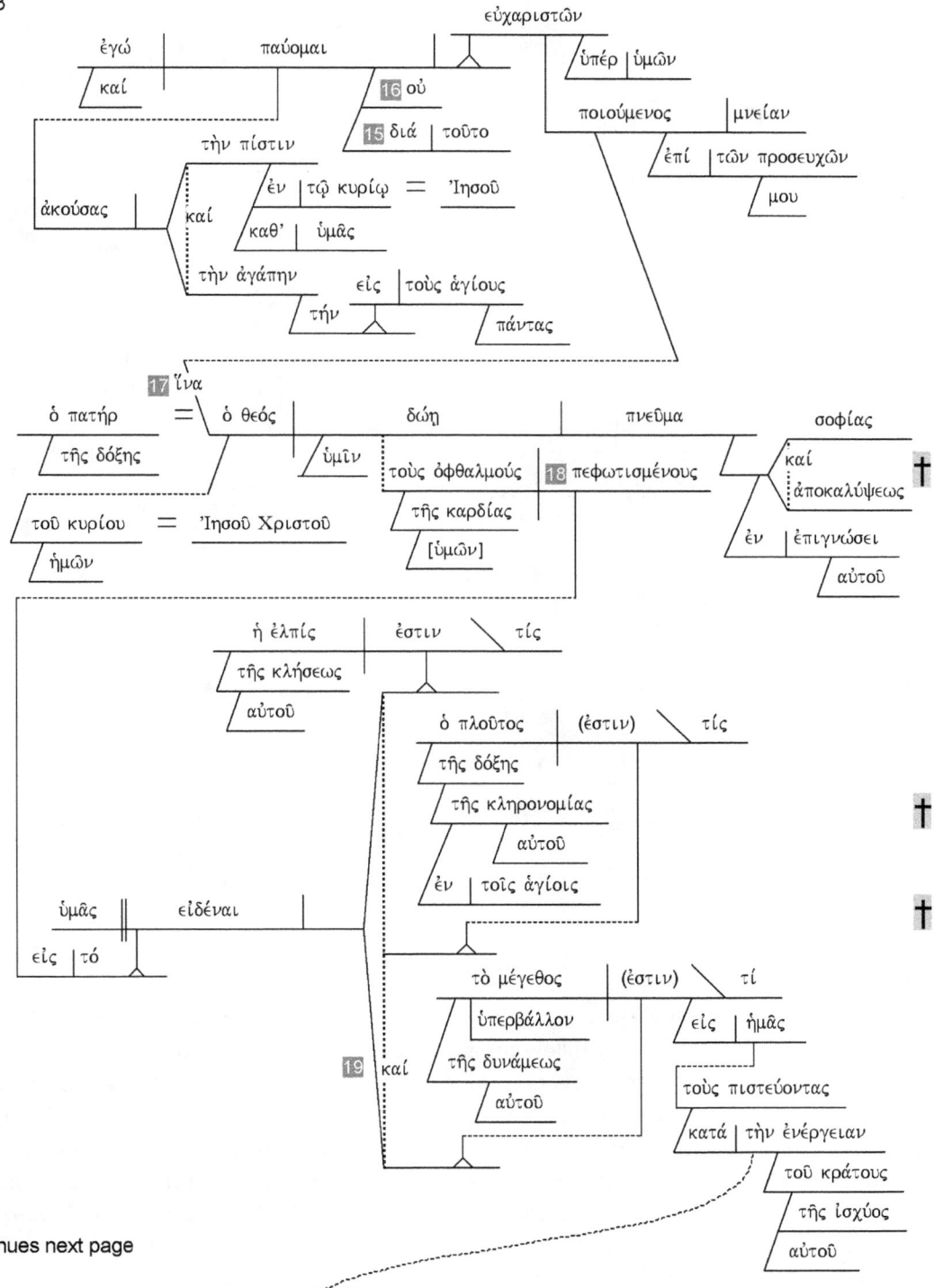

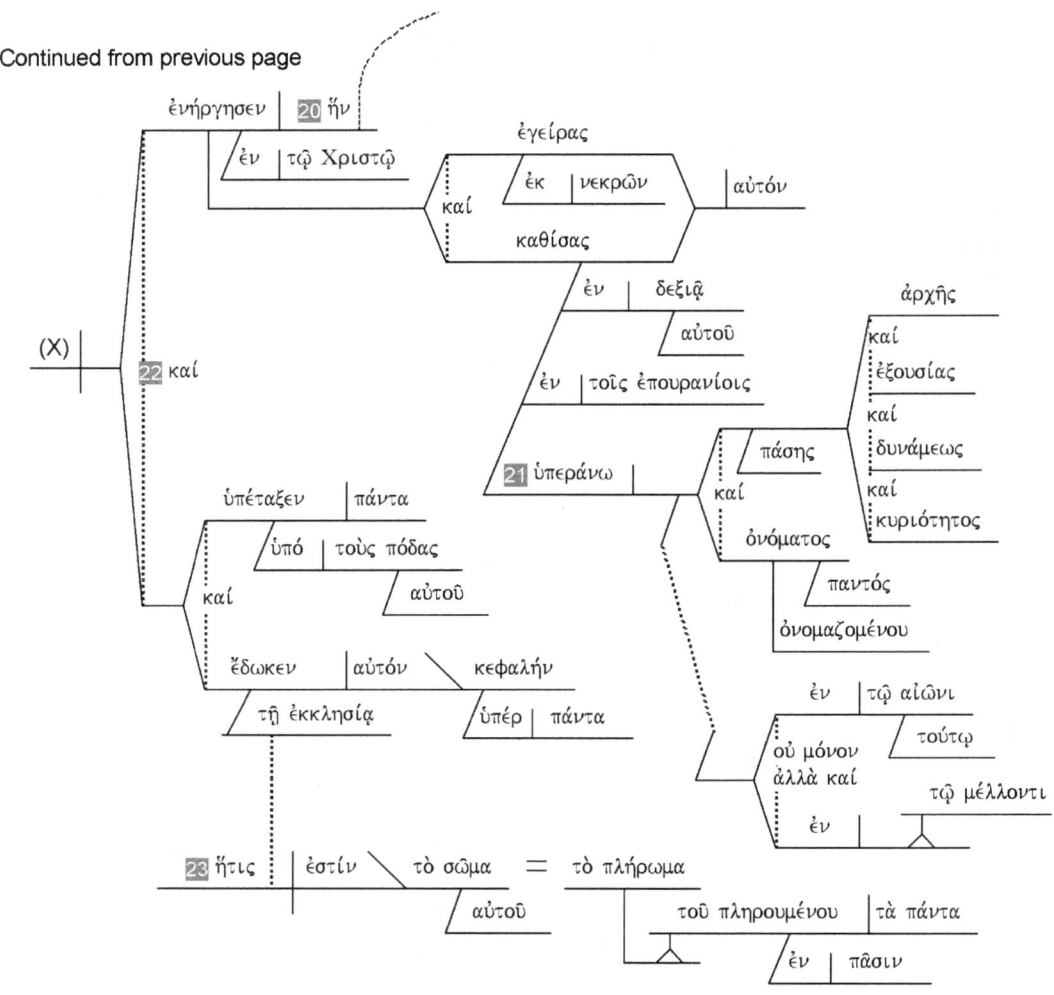

Notes on Ephesians 1

Eph 1:4 ἐν ἀγάπῃ — Many exegetes prefer to construe this phrase with the following material rather than the preceding. I follow the punctuation of NA28 without significant hesitation, believing that the evidence favoring the construction shown in the diagram is no weaker than that favoring the alternative. To any who may be inclined to think that a believer's lifestyle pattern has nothing to do with his unblemished standing before God, I would suggest a careful reading of Paul's statements about love elsewhere (especially Phi 1:9-11), along with 1Jo 4:16-17. Those who choose to construe the phrase with verse 5 may well be correct, but, in my opinion at least, there is nothing theologically inferior about construing it with verse 4. It is also possible to construe the phrase with v. 4 and still take it as referring to God's love: we stand blameless before him in the sphere of (or because of) his love.

Eph 1:8 ἐν πάσῃ σοφίᾳ καὶ φρονήσει — The versions are divided over whether to construe this phrase with what precedes or with what follows. The punctuation of NA28 is ambiguous. A clear sequence of thought can be made out either way. The interpretation of this phrase and of the phrase ἐν ἀγάπῃ in verse 4 may well be related. I am consistently construing each with the preceding material rather than with the participle that follows; others may wish to do the opposite in both cases.

Eph 1:13 ἐν ᾧ (second occurrence) — The phrase could alternatively be construed as a simple repetition of the first occurrence, which modifies ἐσφραγίσθητε.

Eph 1:18 τοὺς ὀφθαλμούς — This noun could also be construed as a second object of δώῃ, with πεφωτισμένους functioning as object complement.

Eph 1:18 εἰδέναι — The infinitive phrase could alternatively be construed as modifying δώῃ.

Eph 1:18 κληρονομίας — The genitive could alternatively be construed as modifying πλοῦτος.

2:1-6 EPHESIANS

2:1-7

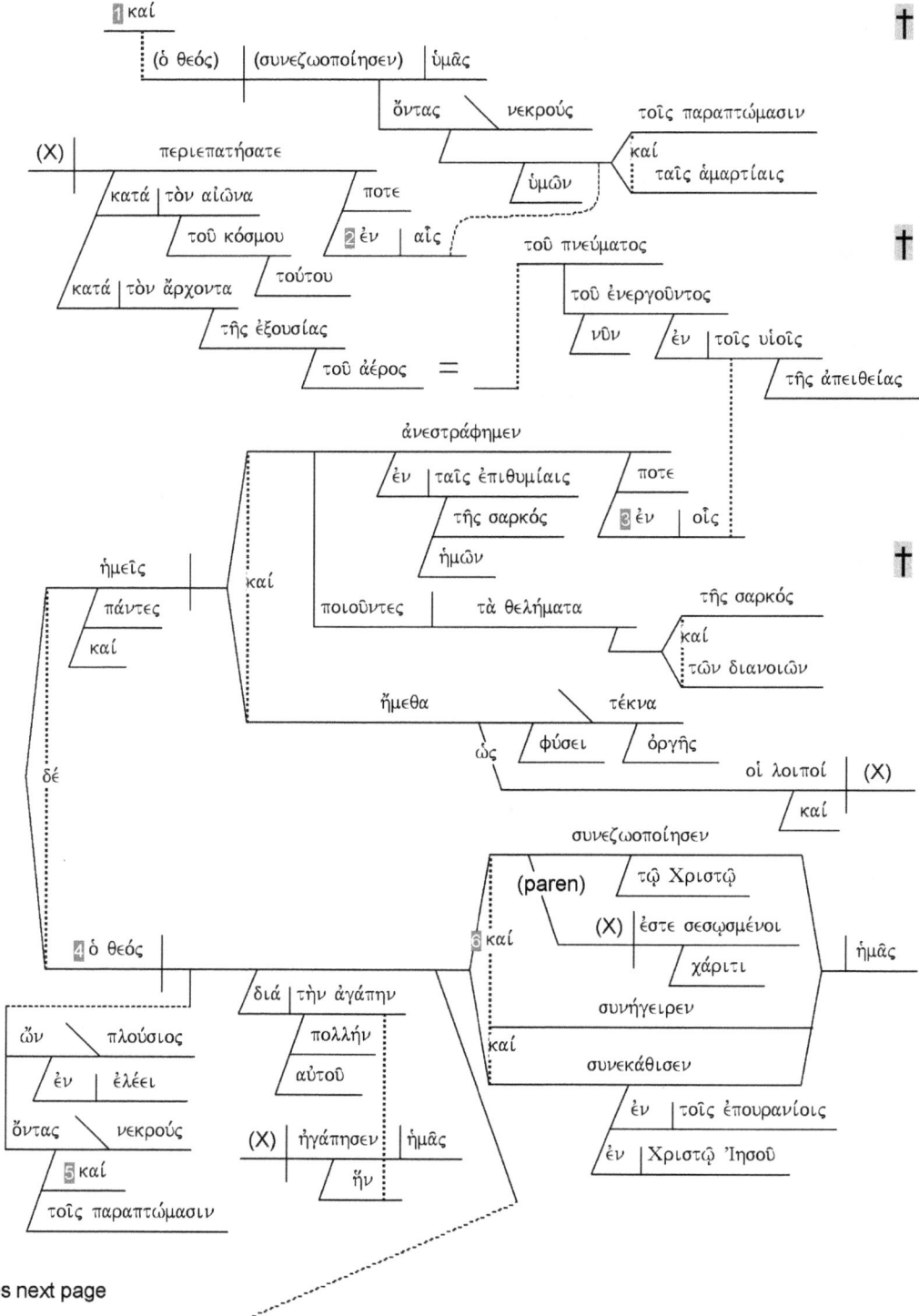

Continues next page

Continued from previous page

2:8-9

2:10

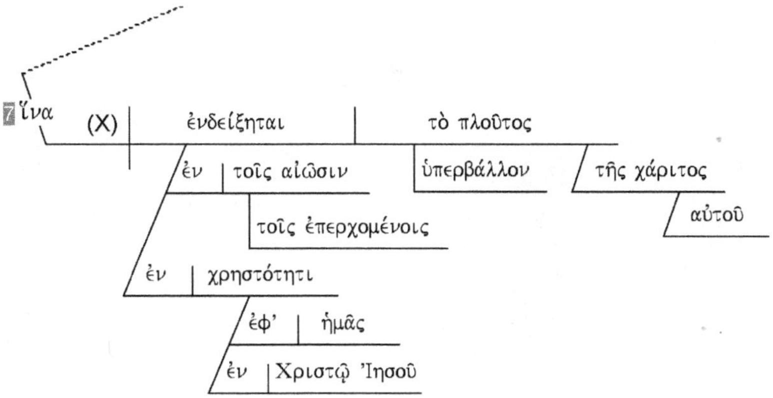

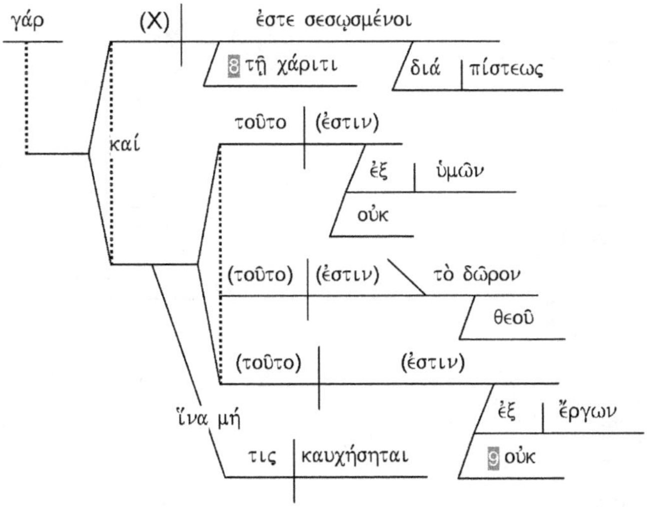

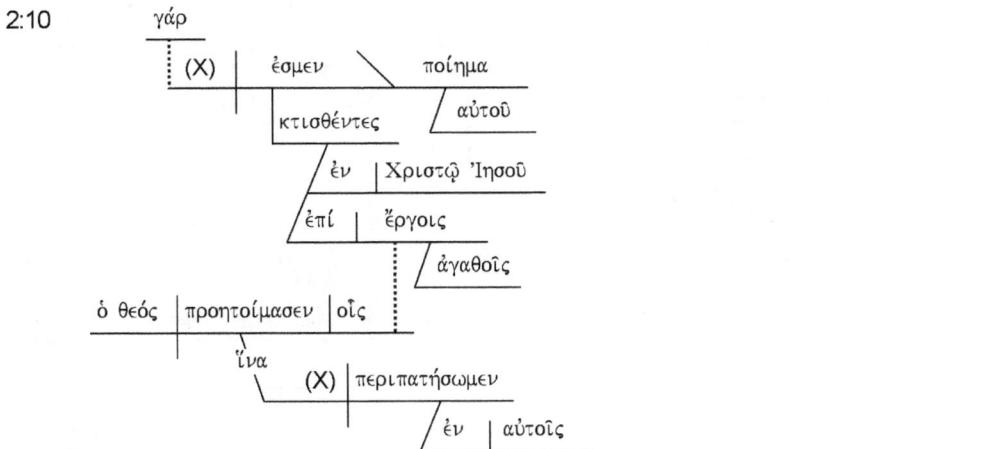

2:11-16 EPHESIANS

2:11-12

2:13

2:14-16

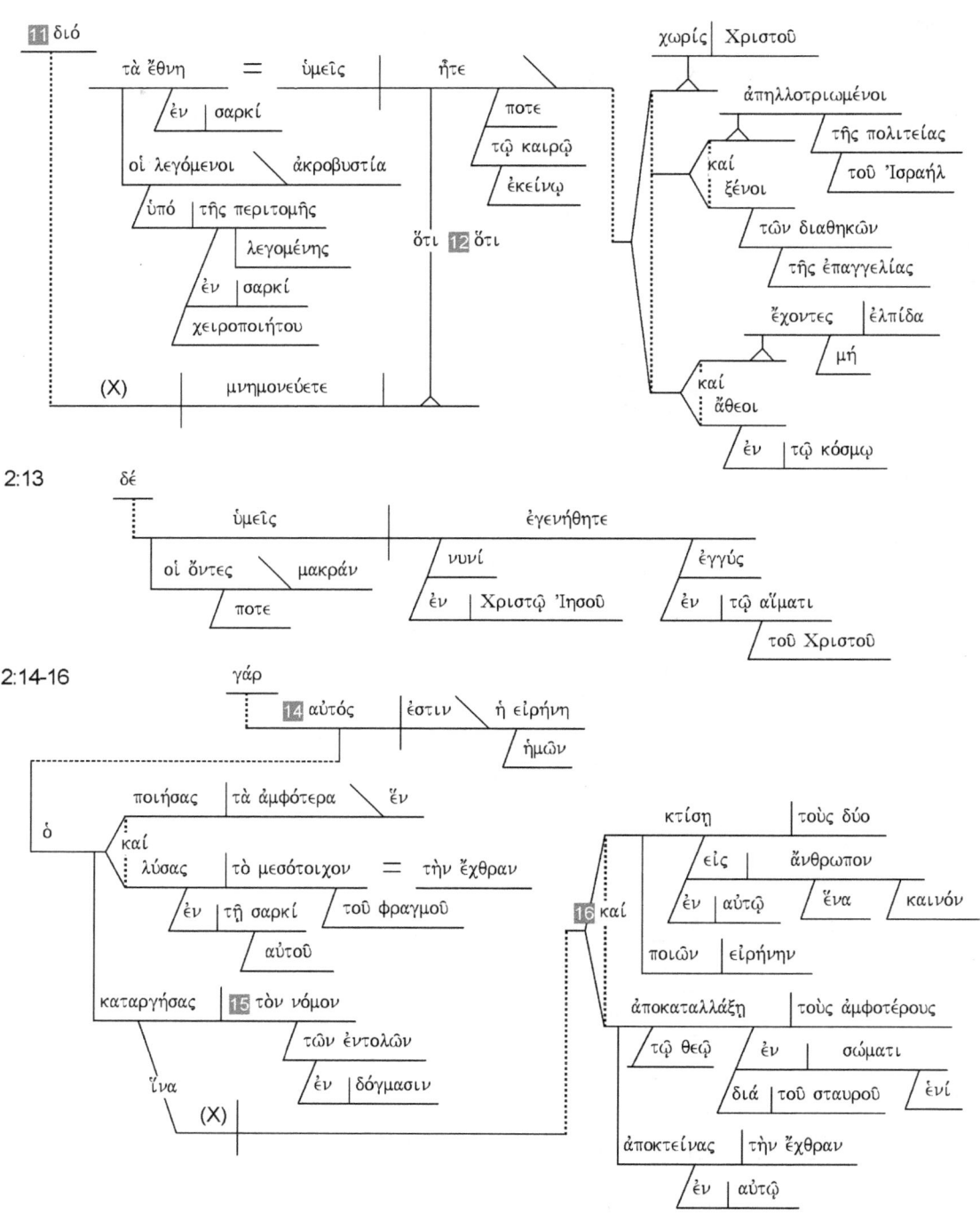

EPHESIANS 2:17-22

2:17-18

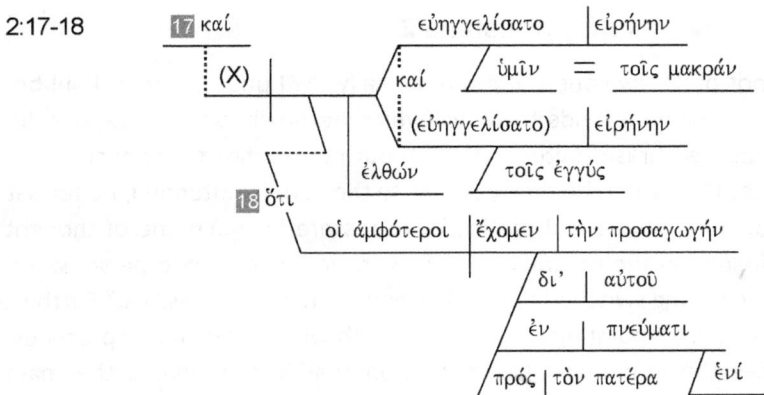

2:19-22

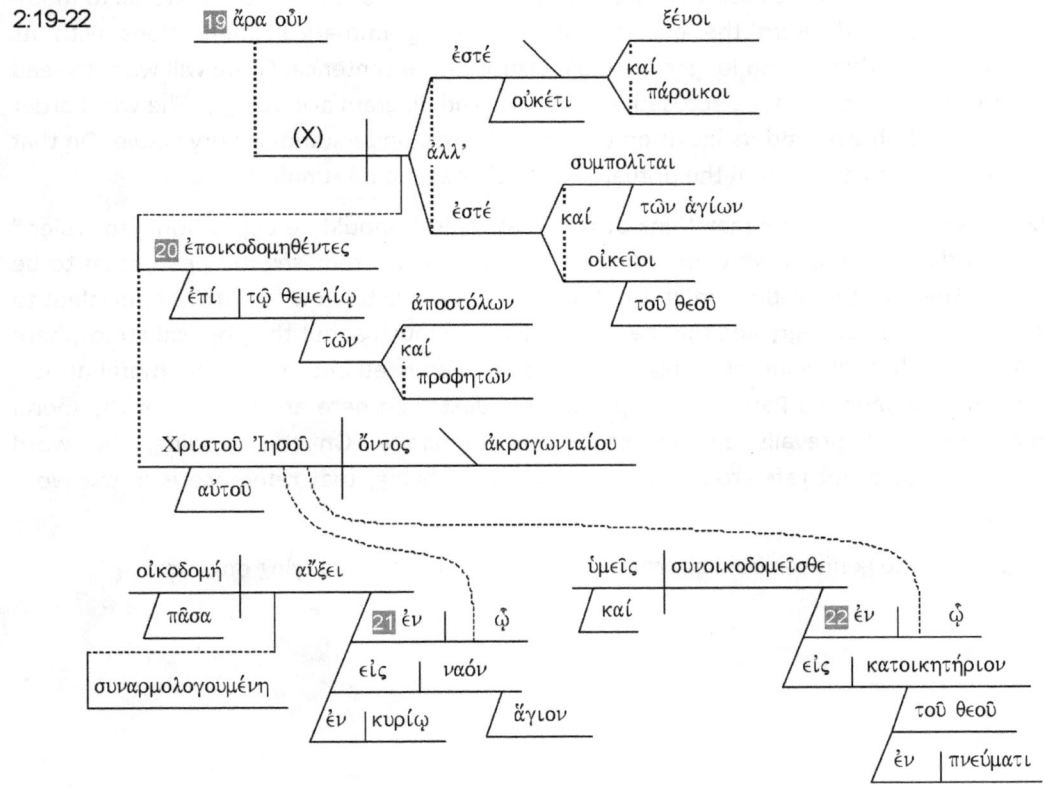

25

Notes on Ephesians 2

Eph 2:1-7 — The sentence is not perfectly coherent grammatically. As I understand it, Paul begins with the object of the verb he intends to write (which he finally does write in v. 5), attaching an adverbial participle phrase (ὄντας νεκρούς). But he expands so extensively on the idea of being dead in sins that, when he finally comes to the verb he intended, he feels it necessary to restate the opening object and participle, to restore his main line of thought for the reader/hearer to follow. In the meanwhile, however, he has switched persons: initially he had "you," but now, having switched to the first person in v. 3, he has "us." Further, he tosses in a conjunction (δέ, v. 4), pointing up a contrast with what immediately precedes. This conjunction introduces the grammatical complication that it coordinates the main clause Paul originally intended with a subordinate clause he developed in the process of working up to the main one. It seemed to me that the best way to diagram was simply to supply an elliptical main clause with minimal elements for the subordinate material to modify, and then to diagram the explicit clause in its grammatical connections with its surroundings so that it is no longer the main clause of the sentence. Some will want to read the ὄντας νεκρούς phrases as accusative absolutes and diagram accordingly. The word order of the second phrase, and its inclusion of καί, make this understanding very viable. On that reading, an elliptical object of the primary verbs will have to be supplied.

Eph 2:2 τοῦ πνεύματος — One may think at first that "spirit" should be appositional to "ruler," but I am diagramming strictly according to the case, which requires the head noun to be genitive. Upon further reflection, it is not at all unattractive to view "spirit" as equivalent to "air," and to see Paul signaling that he is not talking so much about the physical atmosphere (though the physical realm probably should not be dismissed entirely) as the moral atmosphere. As I understand Paul's language, Satan is described here as the ruler of the moral atmosphere that prevails among disobedient humanity. On this reading, the word πνεύματος would not refer to an individual personal being; that reference is in the word ἄρχοντα.

Eph 2:3 ἡμῶν — The genitive could alternatively be construed as modifying σαρκός.

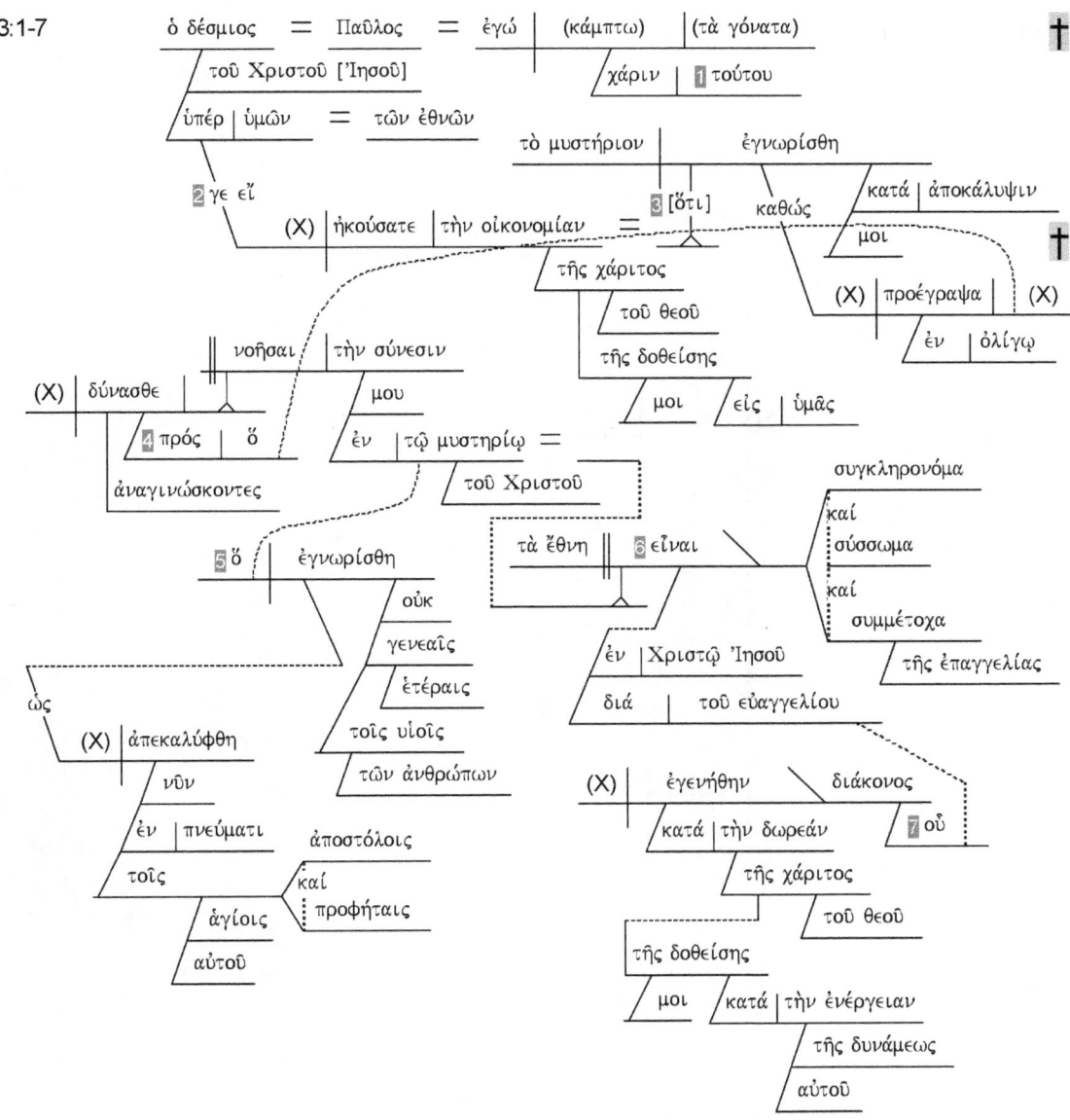

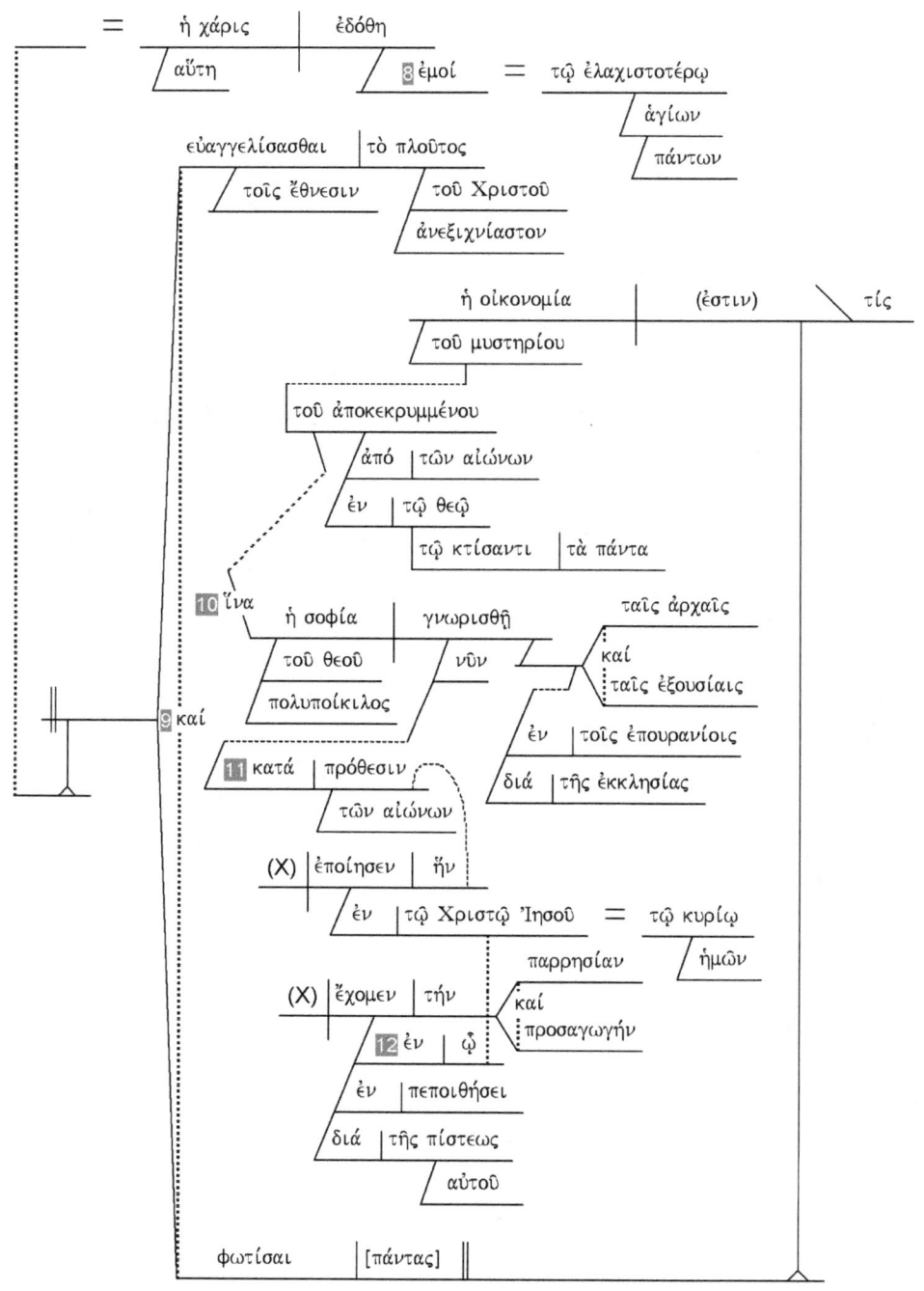

EPHESIANS 3:13-19

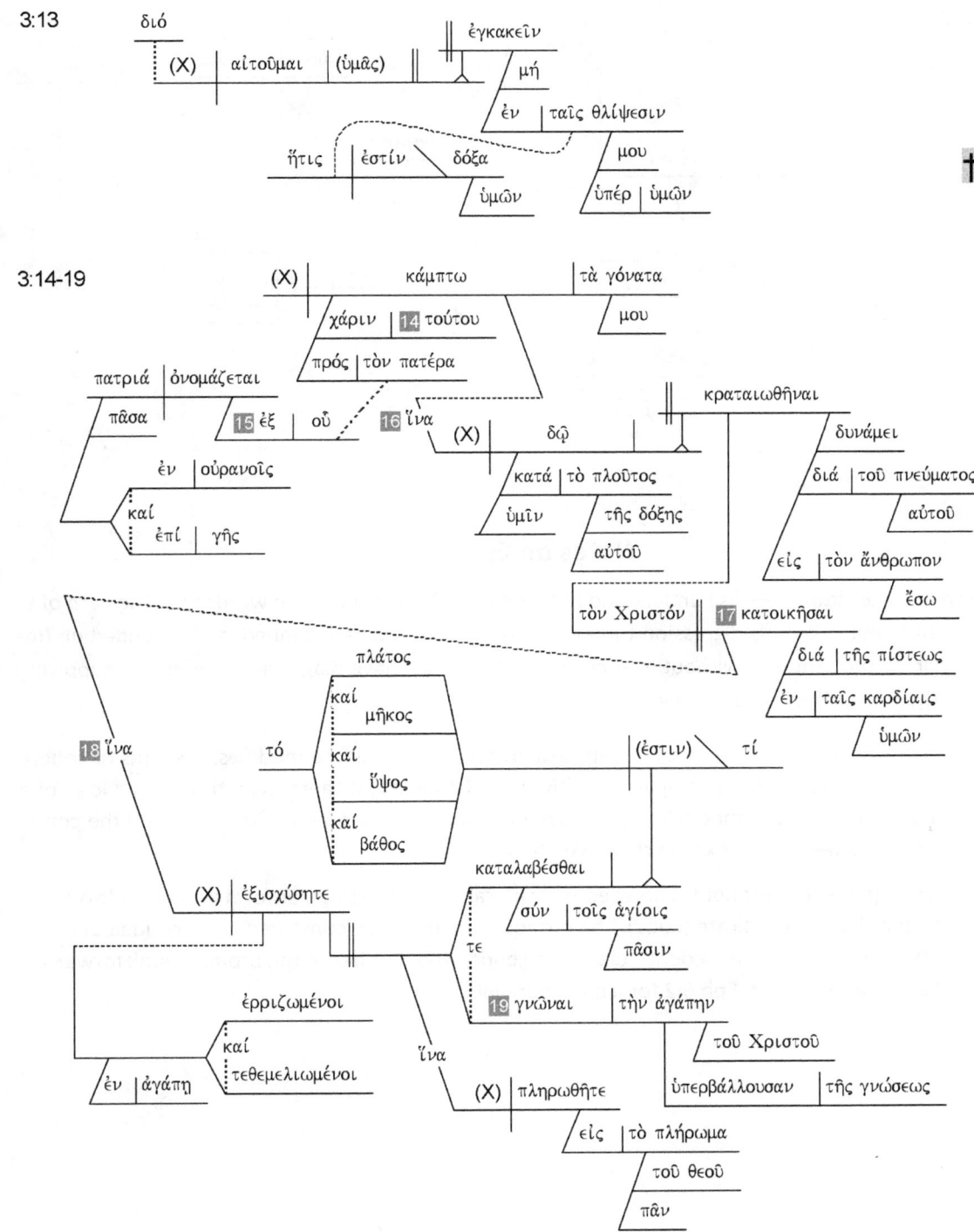

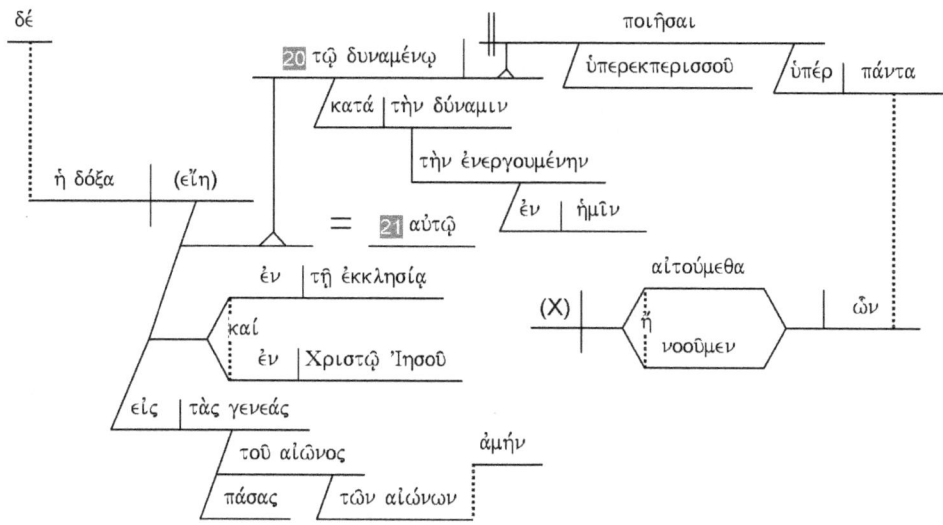

Notes on Ephesians 3

Eph 3:1 ἐγὼ Παῦλος — As I understand the language, Paul wrote these words with the verb of v. 14 in mind, but his digression turned out longer than he had planned, and he ended up finishing the sentence without ever getting to the verb. I have diagrammed by simply supplying the rest of the kernel from v. 14.

Eph 3:2 — It is not at all easy to discern exactly what the εἰ clause modifies. It seems to cohere most naturally with ὑπὲρ ὑμῶν τῶν ἐθνῶν, so I have put it there even though the idea of a subordinate clause modifying a prepositional phrase seems very odd to me, and the conditional element is not exactly clear even here.

Eph 3:13 ἥτις — The pronoun's antecedent is plural; I take the singular form as looking forward to the singular predicate (δόξα). The pronoun could also be construed with the idea of not losing heart as its antecedent. Again, the gender and number of the pronoun look forward to the predicate; cf. Eph 6:2 for a good parallel.

EPHESIANS 4:1-7

4:1-6

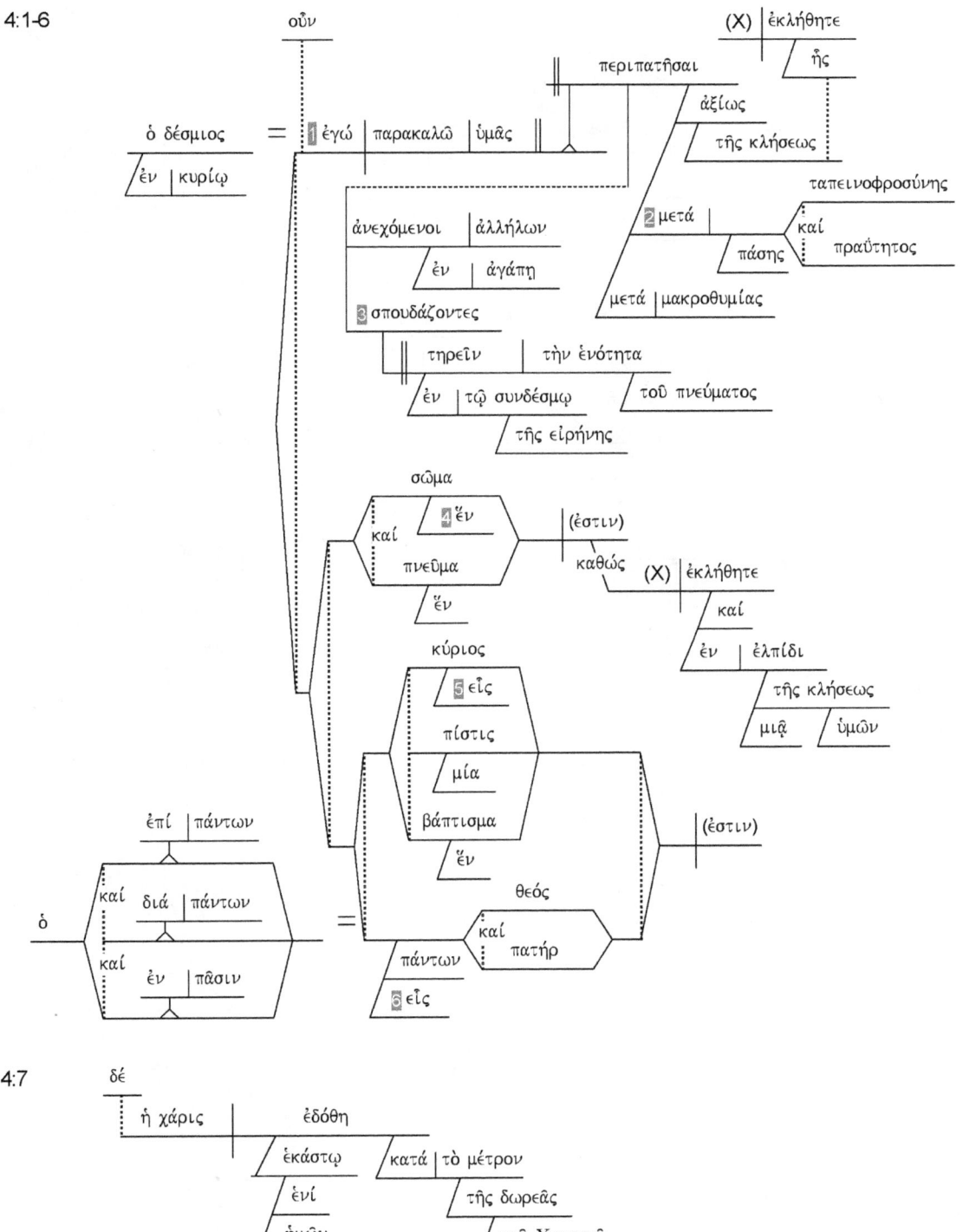

4:8-10 EPHESIANS

4:8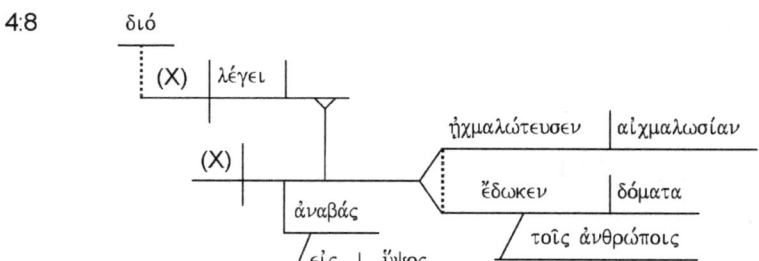

4:9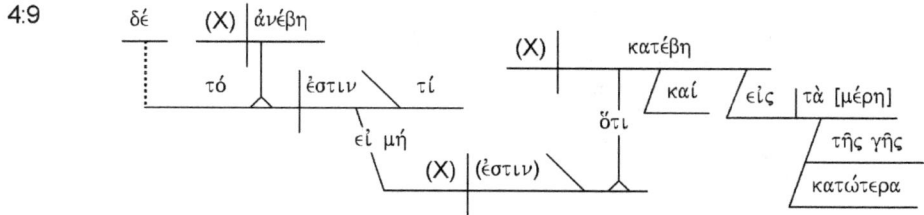

4:10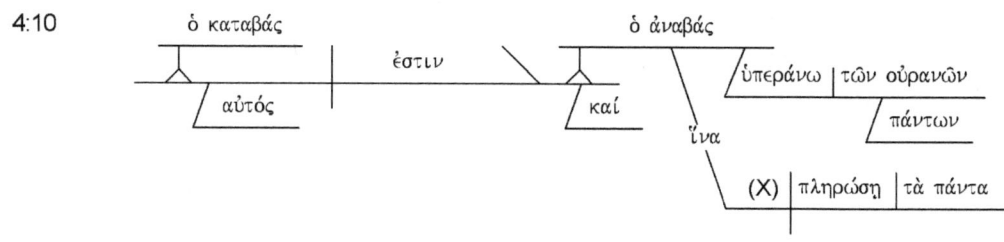

EPHESIANS 4:11-15

4:11-16

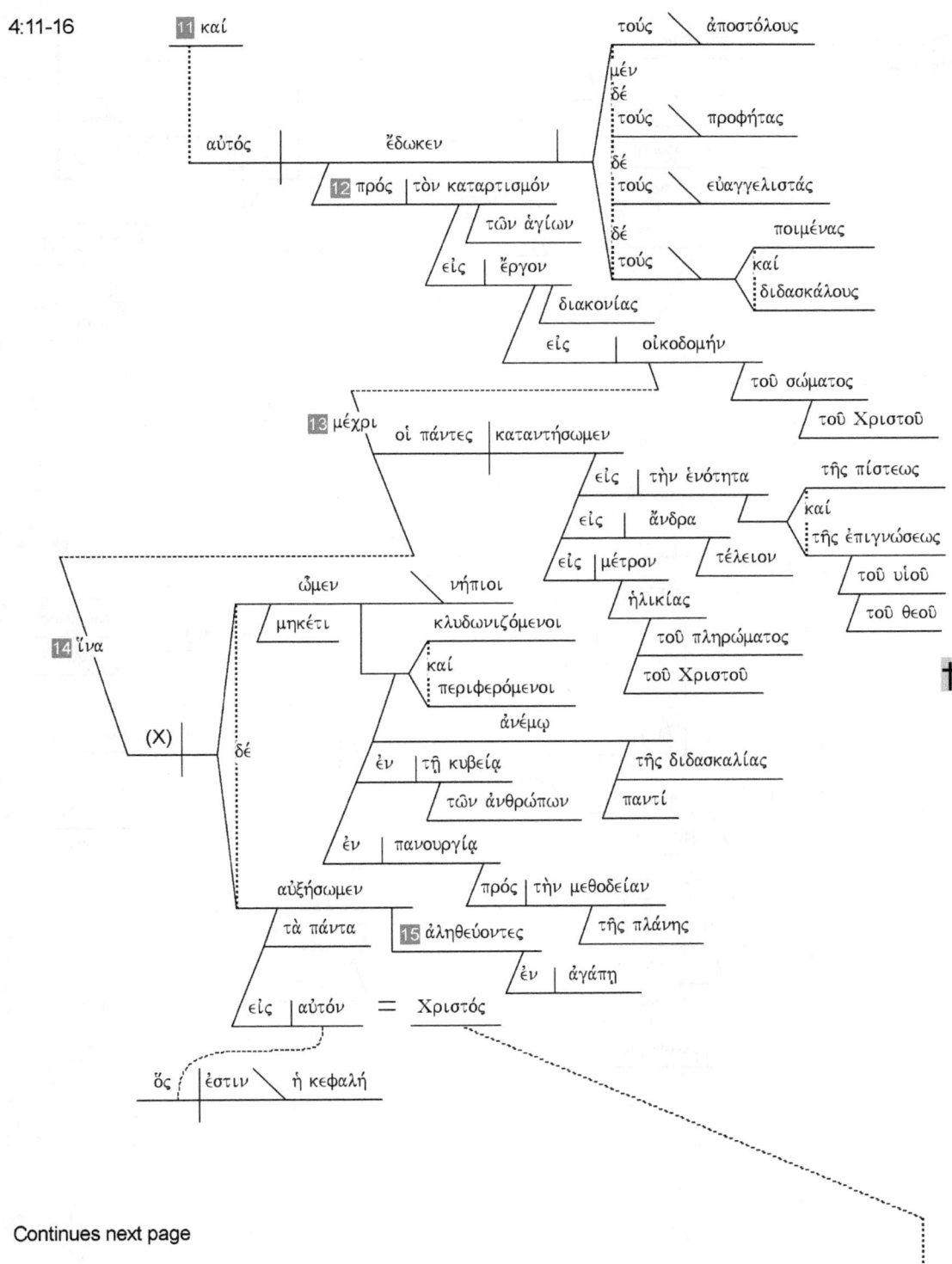

Continues next page

4:16-19 EPHESIANS

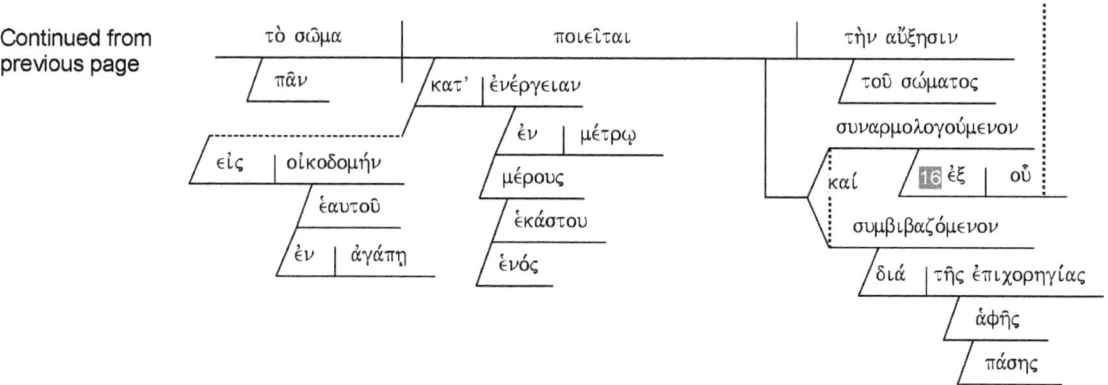

4:17-19

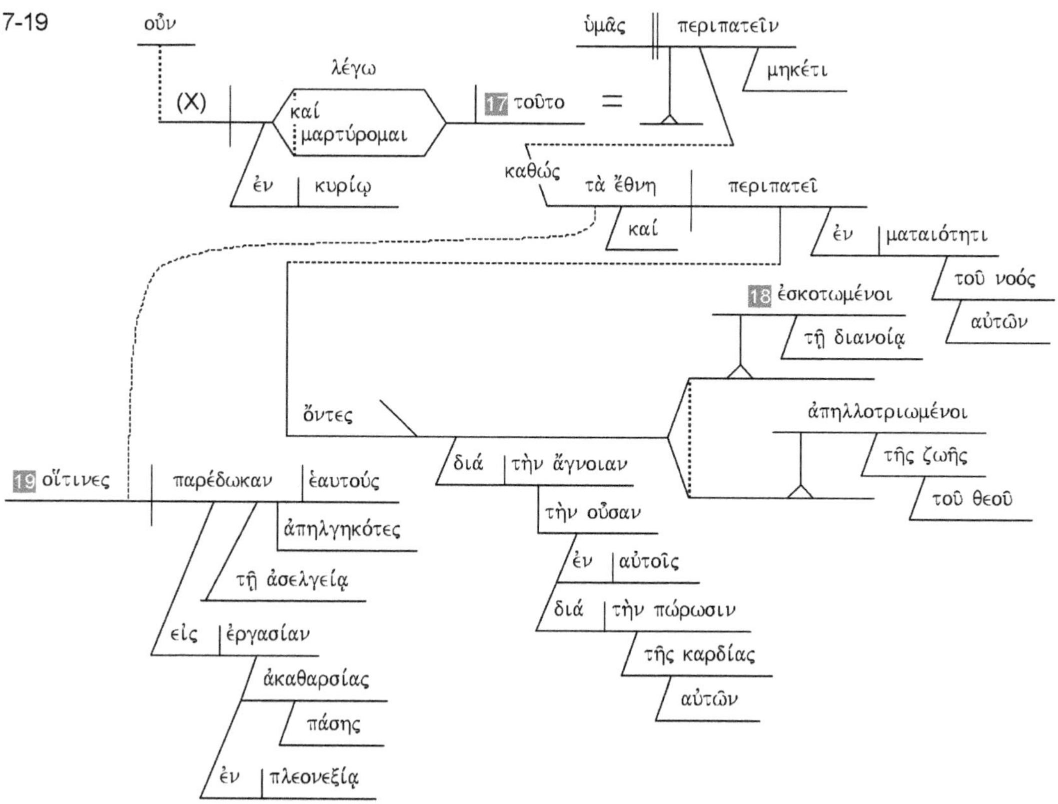

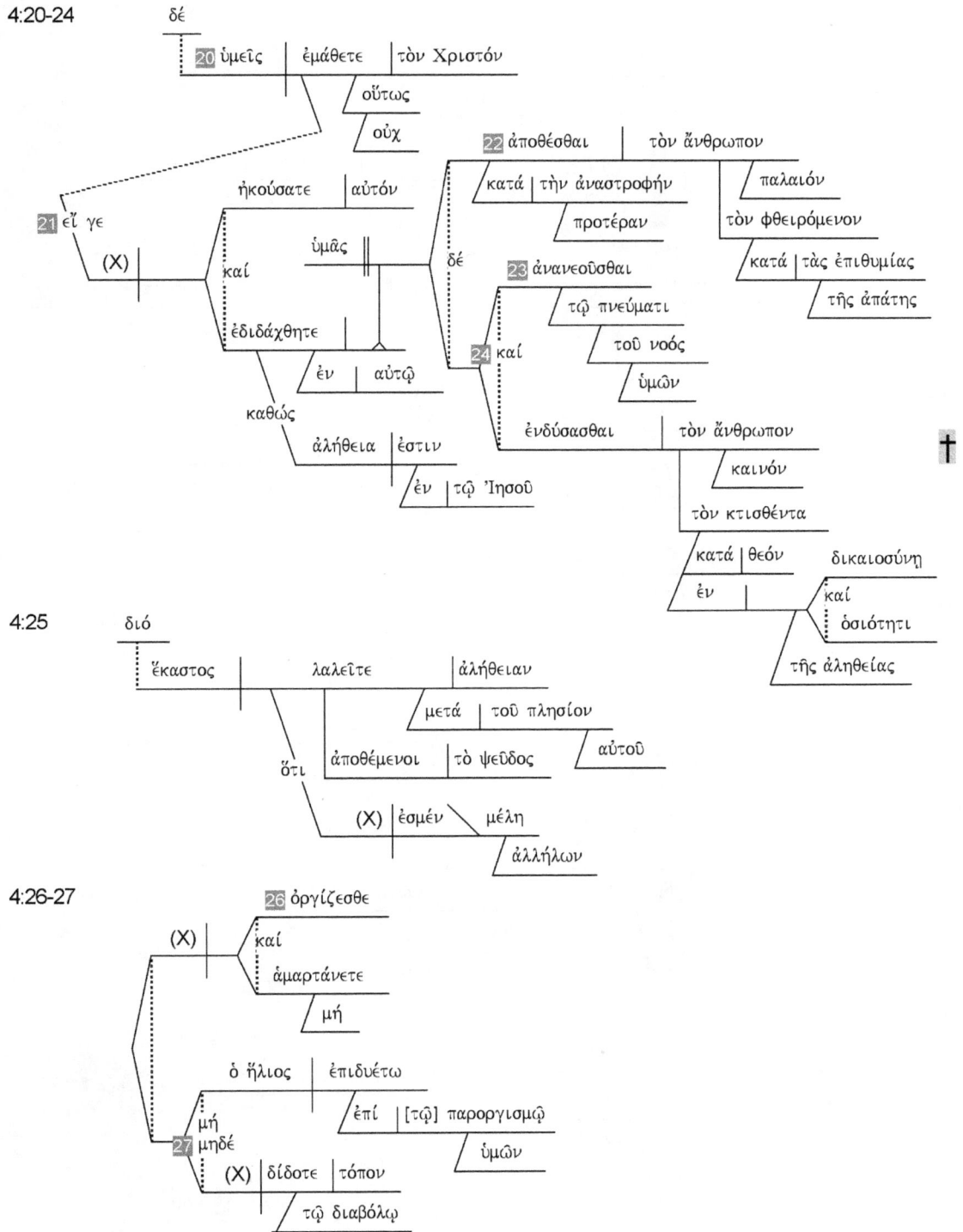

4:28-32 EPHESIANS

4:28
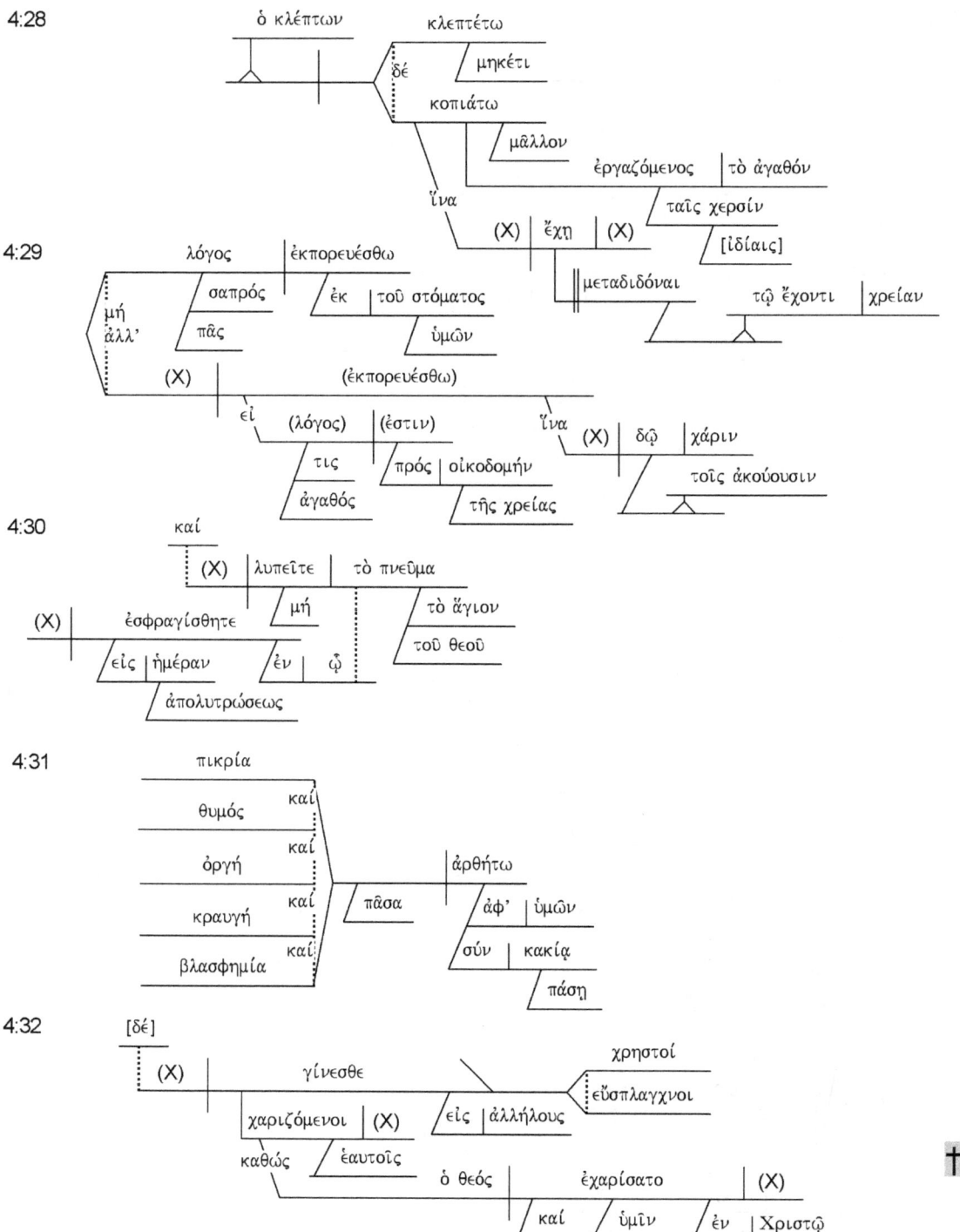

Notes on Ephesians 4

Eph 4:13 τοῦ Χριστοῦ — The genitive could alternatively be construed as modifying πληρώματος.

Eph 4:21 ἀλήθεια — I am inclined to view this noun as the predicate of its clause rather than the subject, the subject being an elliptical repetition of the infinitive phrase "that you put off." The diagram reflects deference to the mass of versions, which all seem to take ἀλήθεια as subject. My view would be translated "as is [the] truth in Jesus, that you put off...." On this reading the three infinitives (ἀποθέσθαι, ἀνανεοῦσθαι, and ἐνδύσασθαι) would be viewed as statements of objective reality rather than as statements of command (the related commands begin in v. 25). If the infinitive phrases construe only with ἐδιδάχθητε, they could be either statements of fact or commands—one can be taught that something is true, or one can be taught that he must do something. But on my view that the infinitive phrases also belong to the clause "as is the truth in Jesus," the command interpretation is not nearly so viable. Facts are the truth, but the idea that a command is the truth is rather strange. The parallel passage in Col 3:9-10 presents the same three actions in language whose only natural interpretation is factual.

Eph 4:32 ἑαυτοῖς and ὑμῖν — Some will want to consider the datives to be direct objects rather than indirect objects.

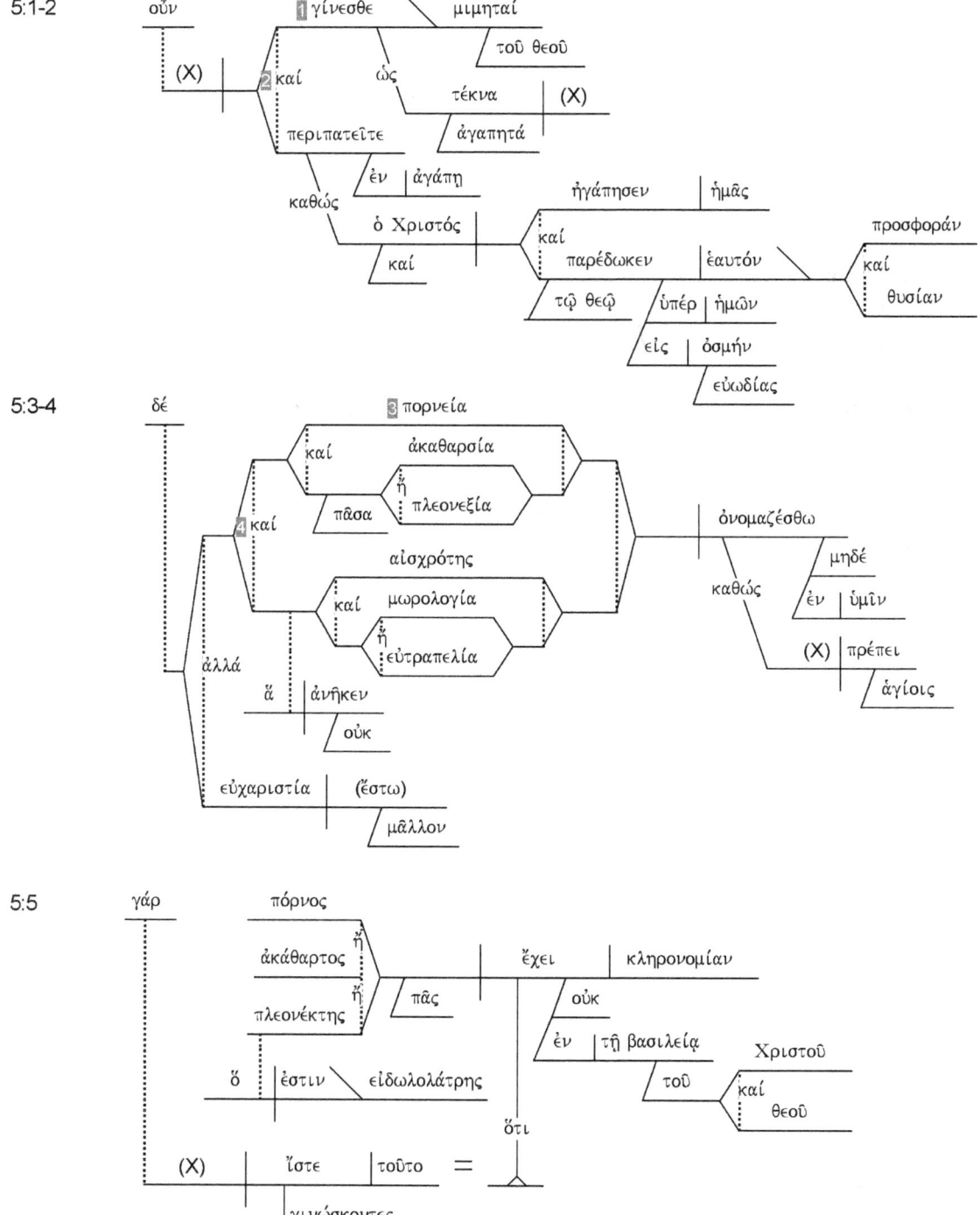

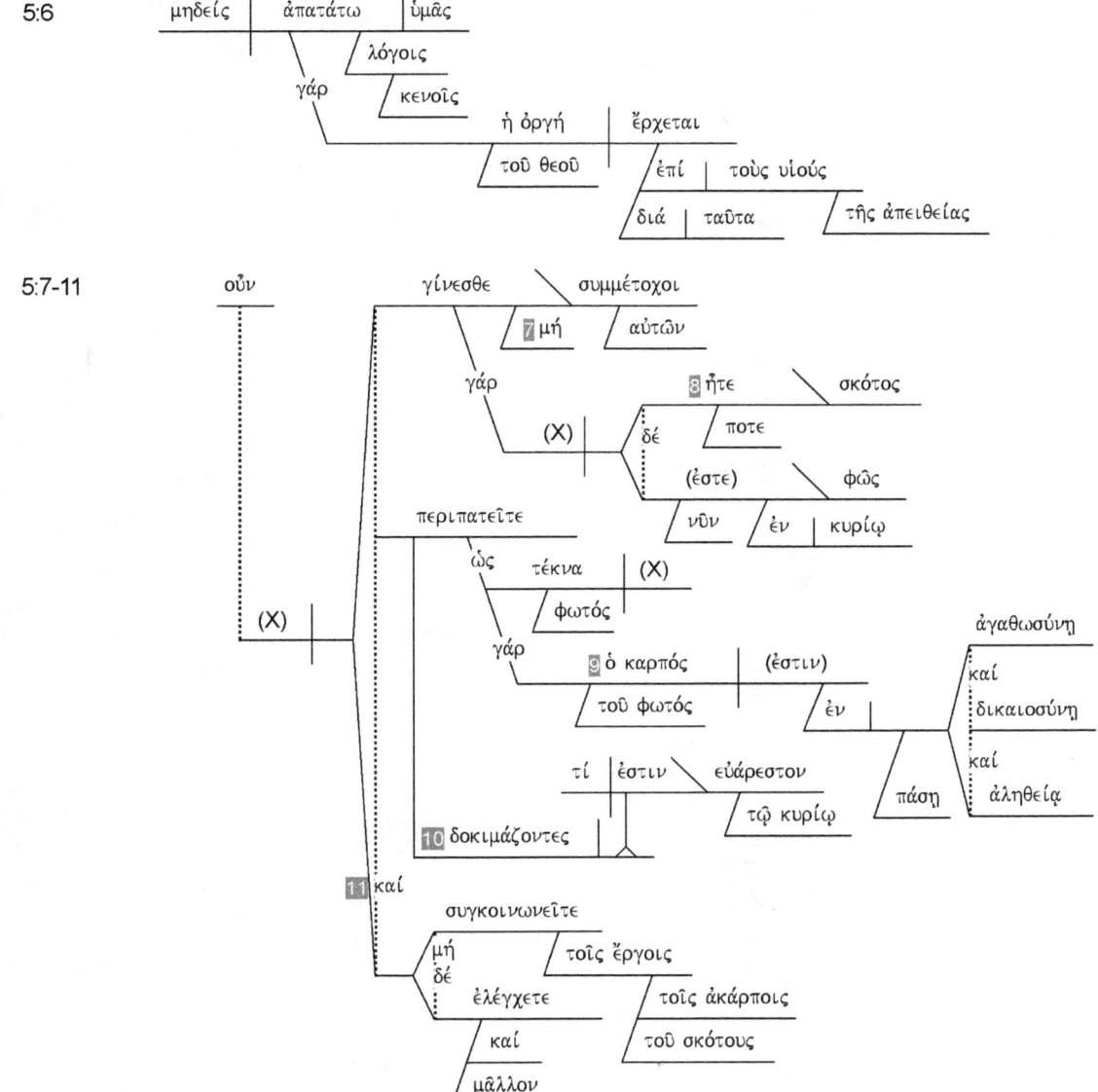

5:12-17

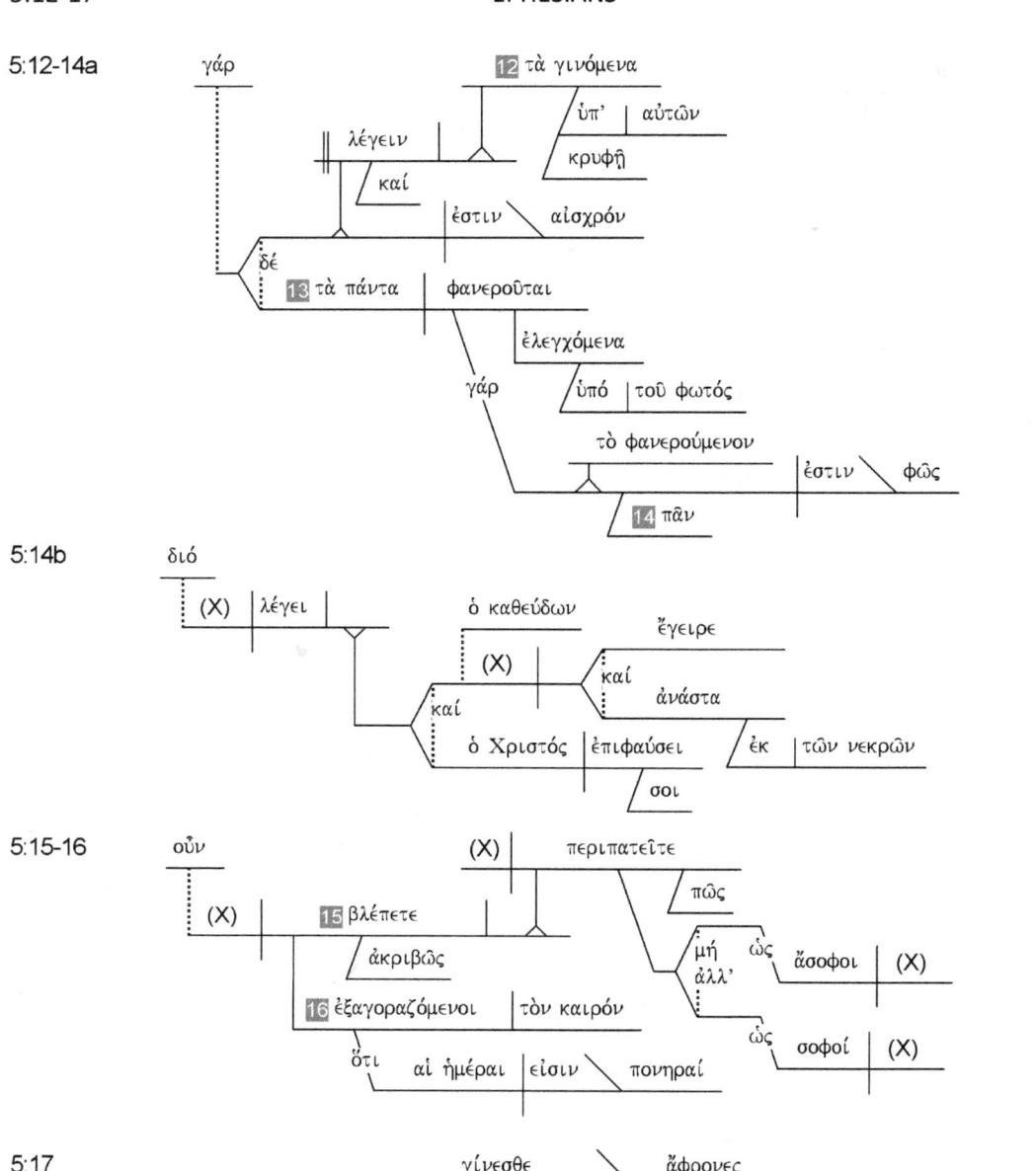

EPHESIANS 5:18-24

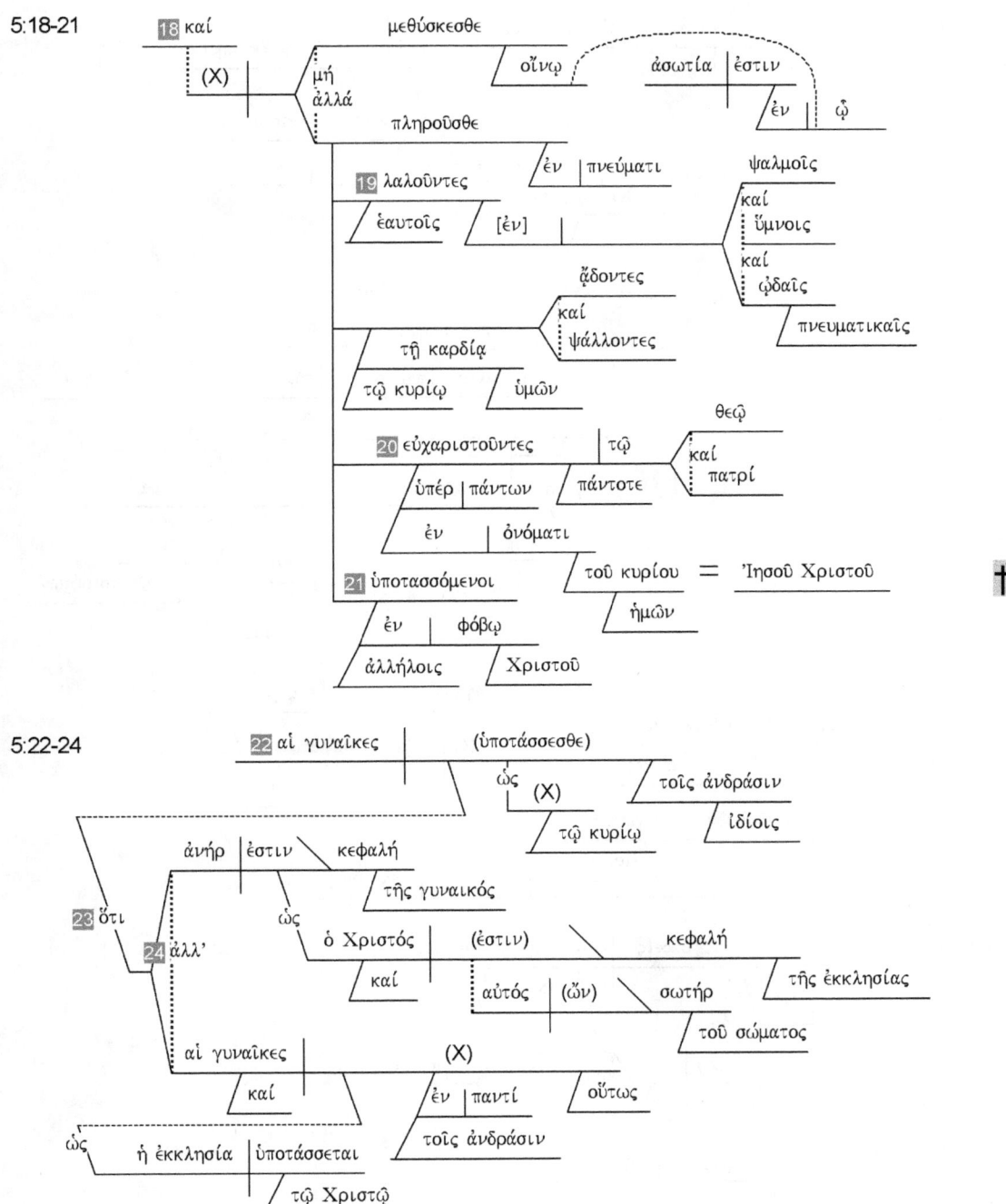

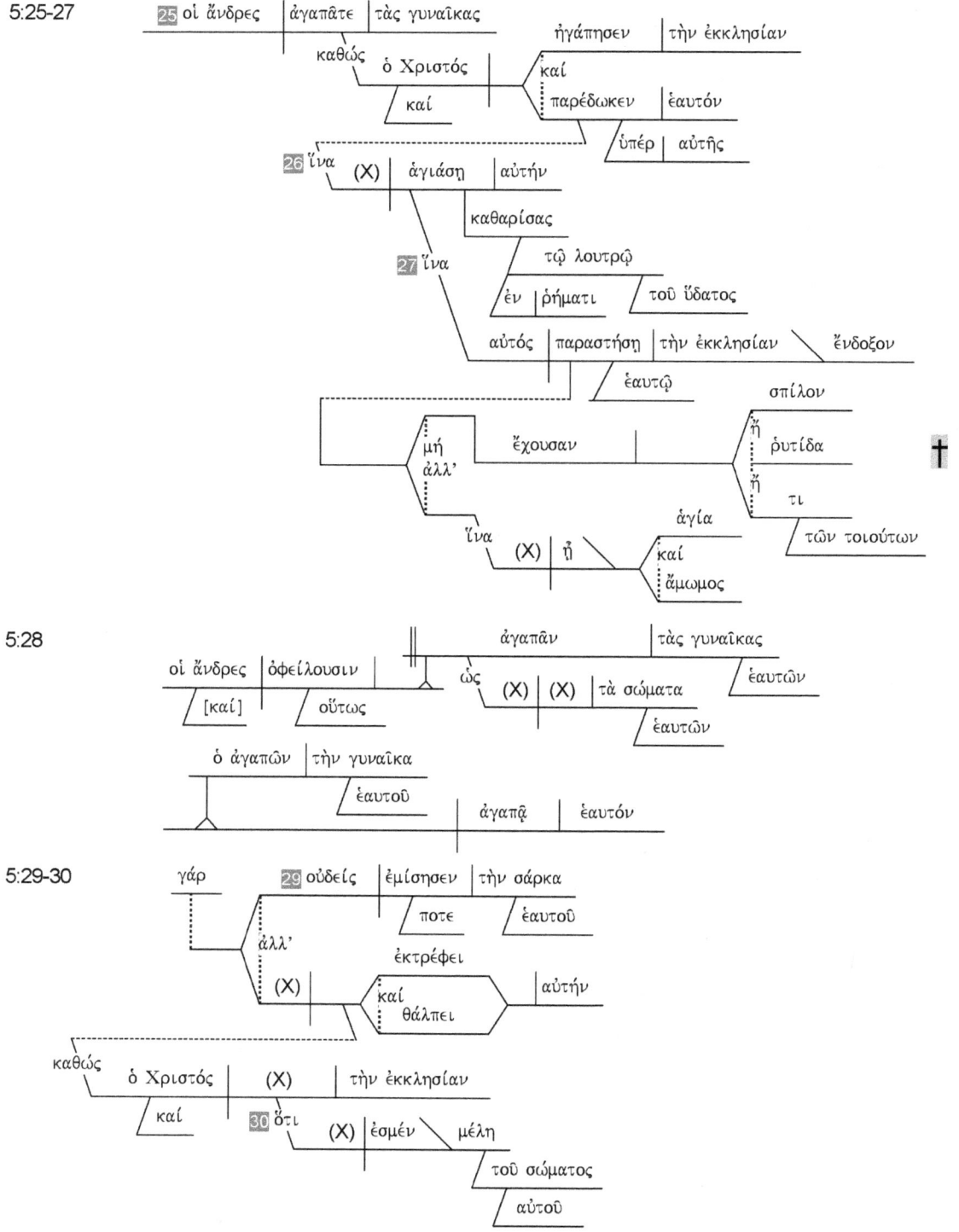

5:31

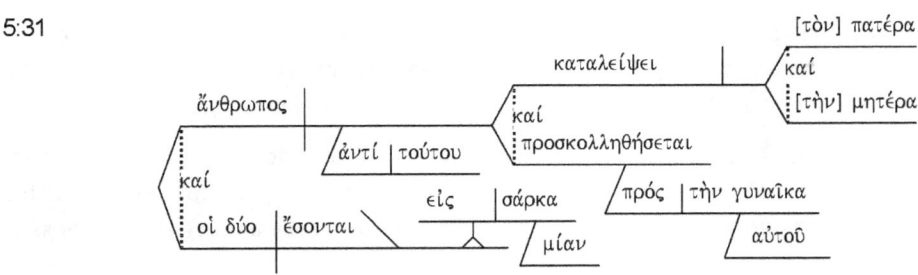

5:32

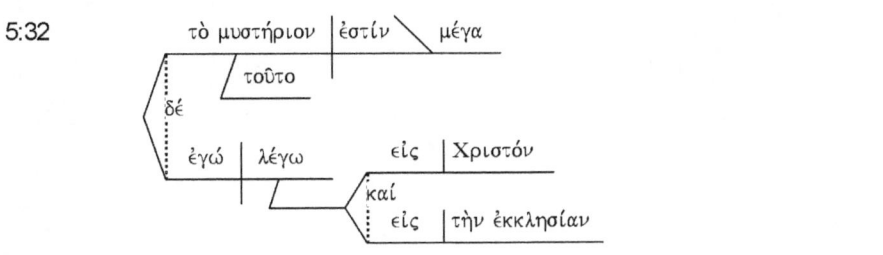

5:33

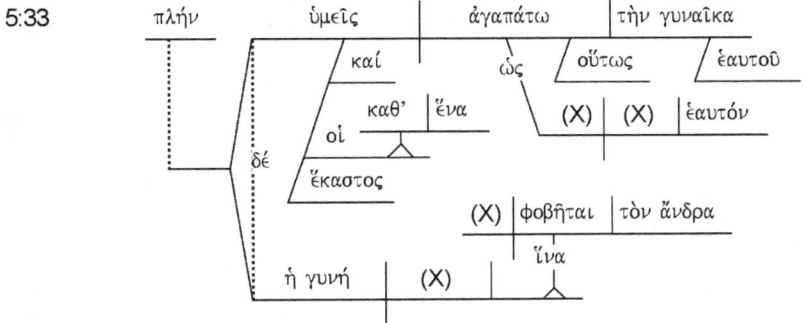

Notes on Ephesians 5

Eph 5:13 πάντα — Some versions take this word as modifying the participle rather than as subject. However, the word order, with πάντα standing between article and the substantival participle that it supposedly modifies, seems unusual. A cursory check for neuter plural participles within 3 words of an agreeing form of πᾶς confirms that the common order for "all the things being reproved" would be πάντα τὰ ἐλεγχόμενα. Hence I have taken the article as governing πάντα rather than the participle, leaving the participle anarthrous and best construed adverbially.

Eph 5:13 ὑπὸ τοῦ φωτός — The prepositional phrase could alternatively be construed as modifying φανεροῦται.

Eph 5:21-22 — I am ignoring NA28's punctuation before v. 21, since v. 21 provides another participle in the series that began in v. 19. Instead, following the versions, I begin the new sentence at v. 22, taking γυναῖκες, in accordance with the pattern followed through the remainder of this section, as the subject of the new sentence (vocative is also possible). In this instance the verb must be supplied elliptically from the immediately preceding context.

Eph 5:27 — The diagramming for the last half of v. 27 looks a little odd, but there is no other way to show the coordination properly. Μή and ἀλλά coordinate a participle phrase with a ἵνα clause whereas ordinarily coordinate elements are grammatically alike. The untidiness of the diagram merely reflects the untidiness of the language.

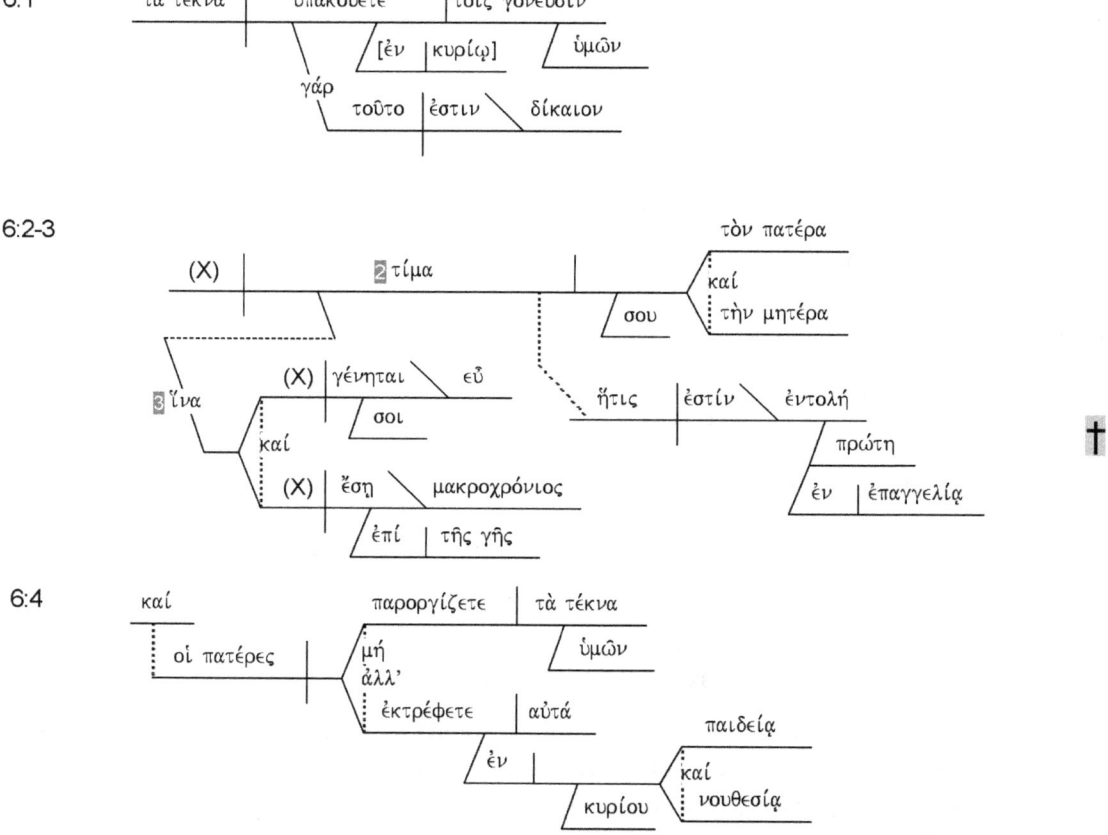

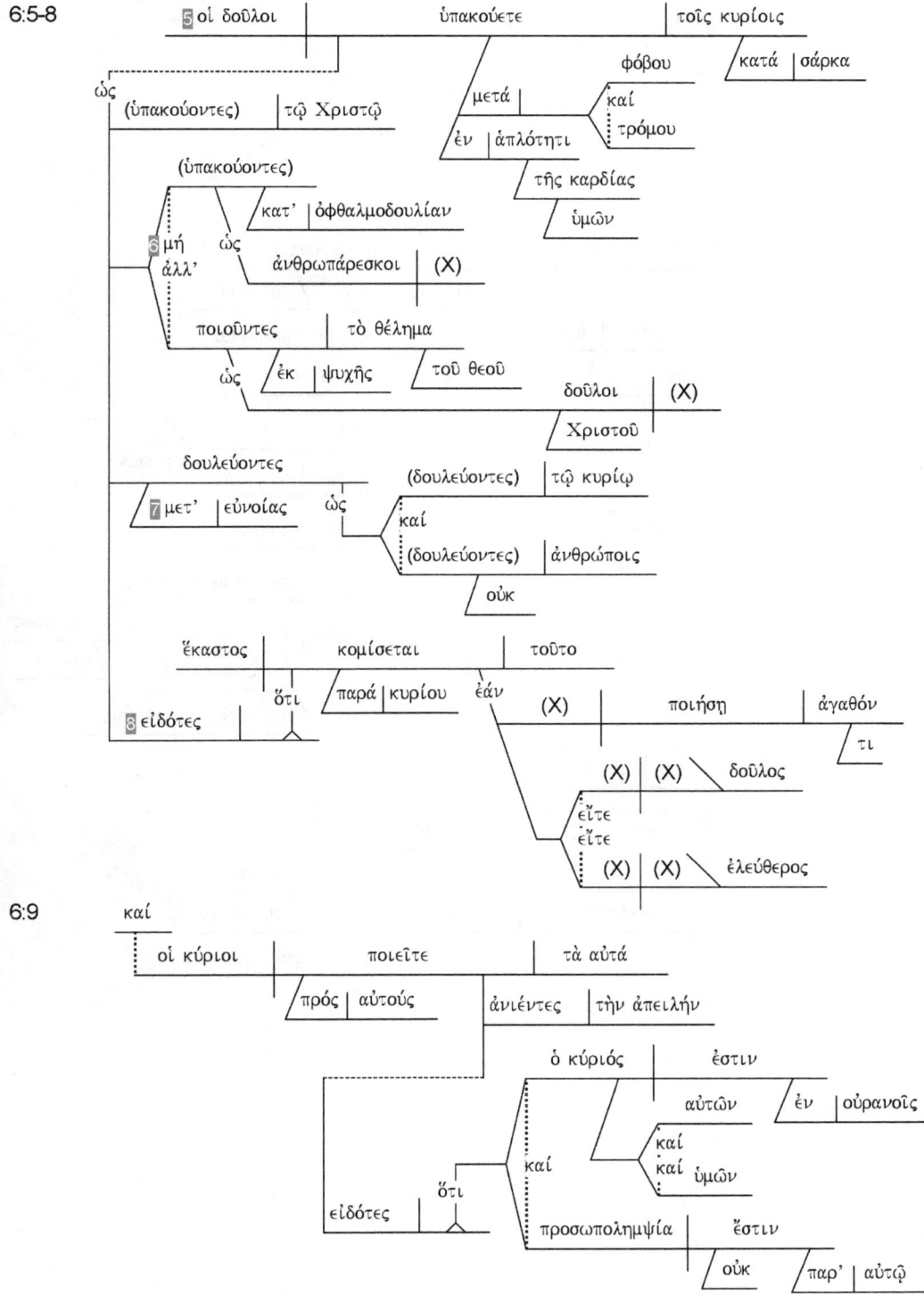

6:10-13 EPHESIANS

6:10

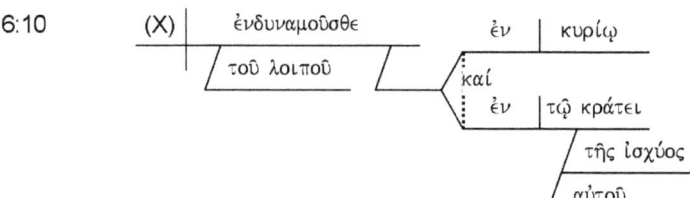

6:11-12

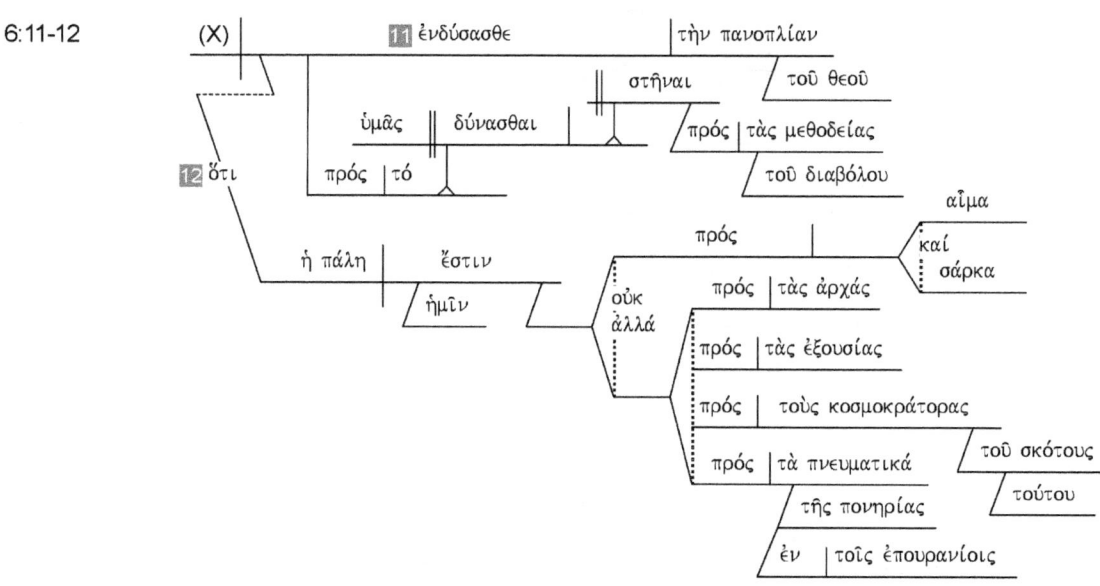

6:13

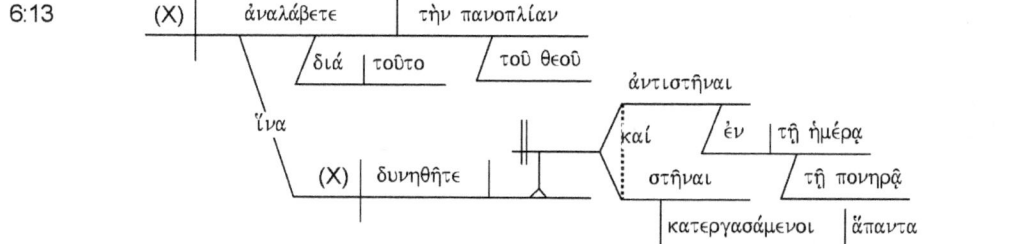

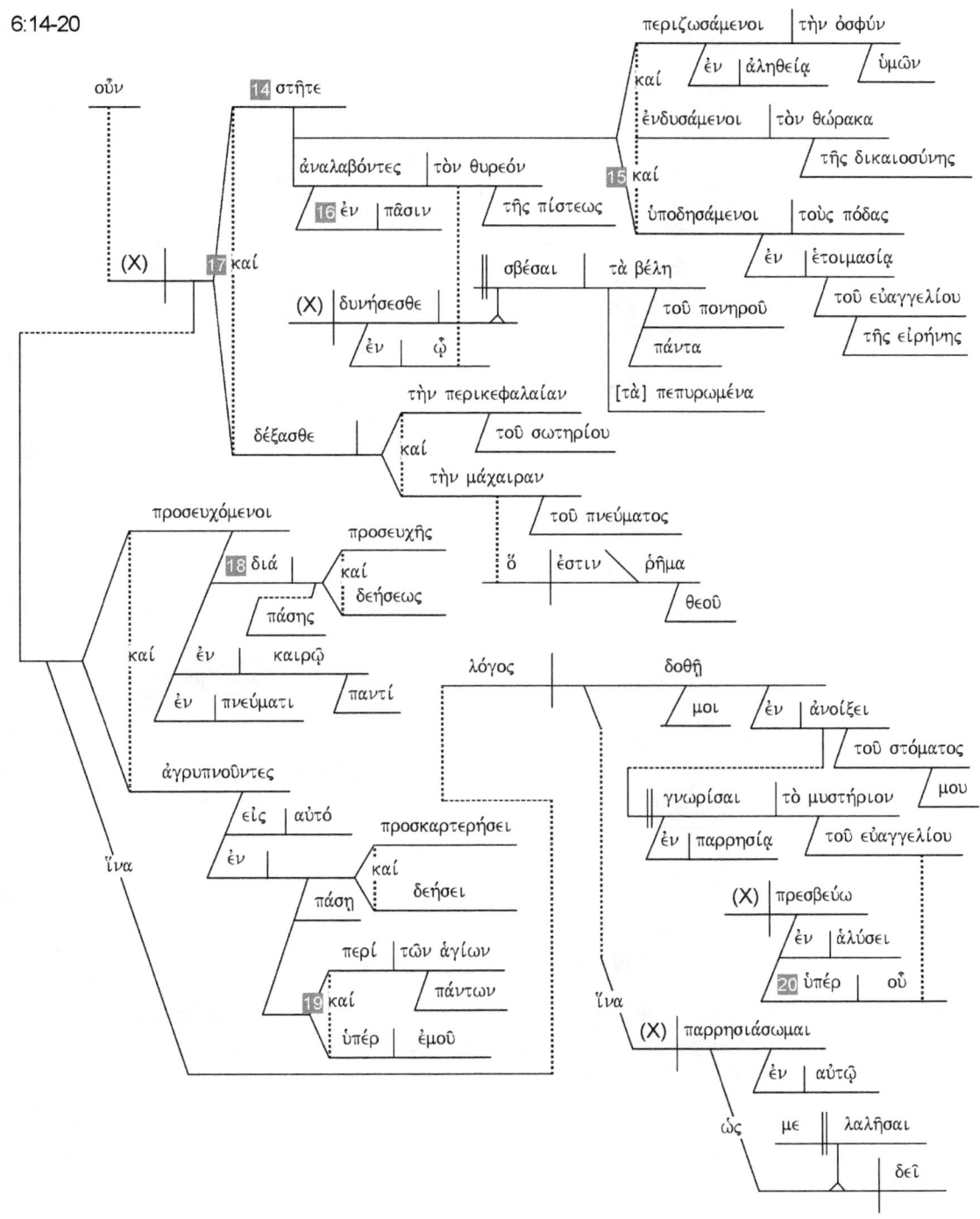

6:21-24

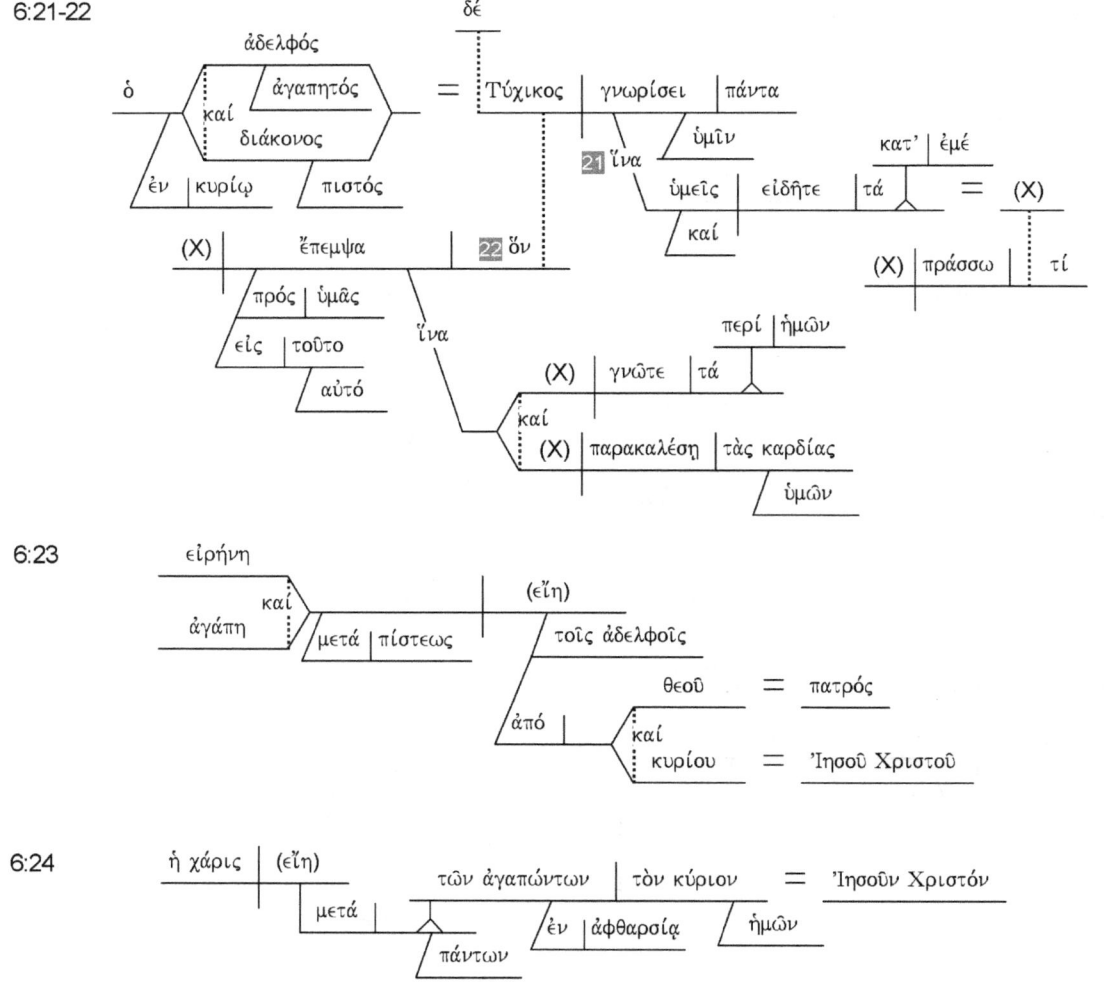

Notes on Ephesians 6

Eph 6:3 — The ἵνα clause could perhaps be diagrammed as a quotation standing in apposition to ἐπαγγελίᾳ, though doing so would lose the purpose connection back to the main clause.

COLOSSIANS

1:1-2

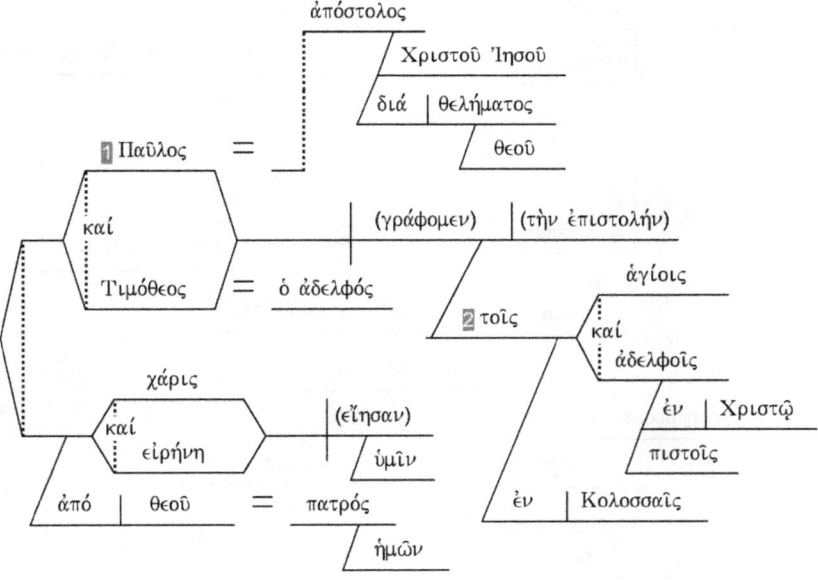

1:3-8 COLOSSIANS

1:3-8

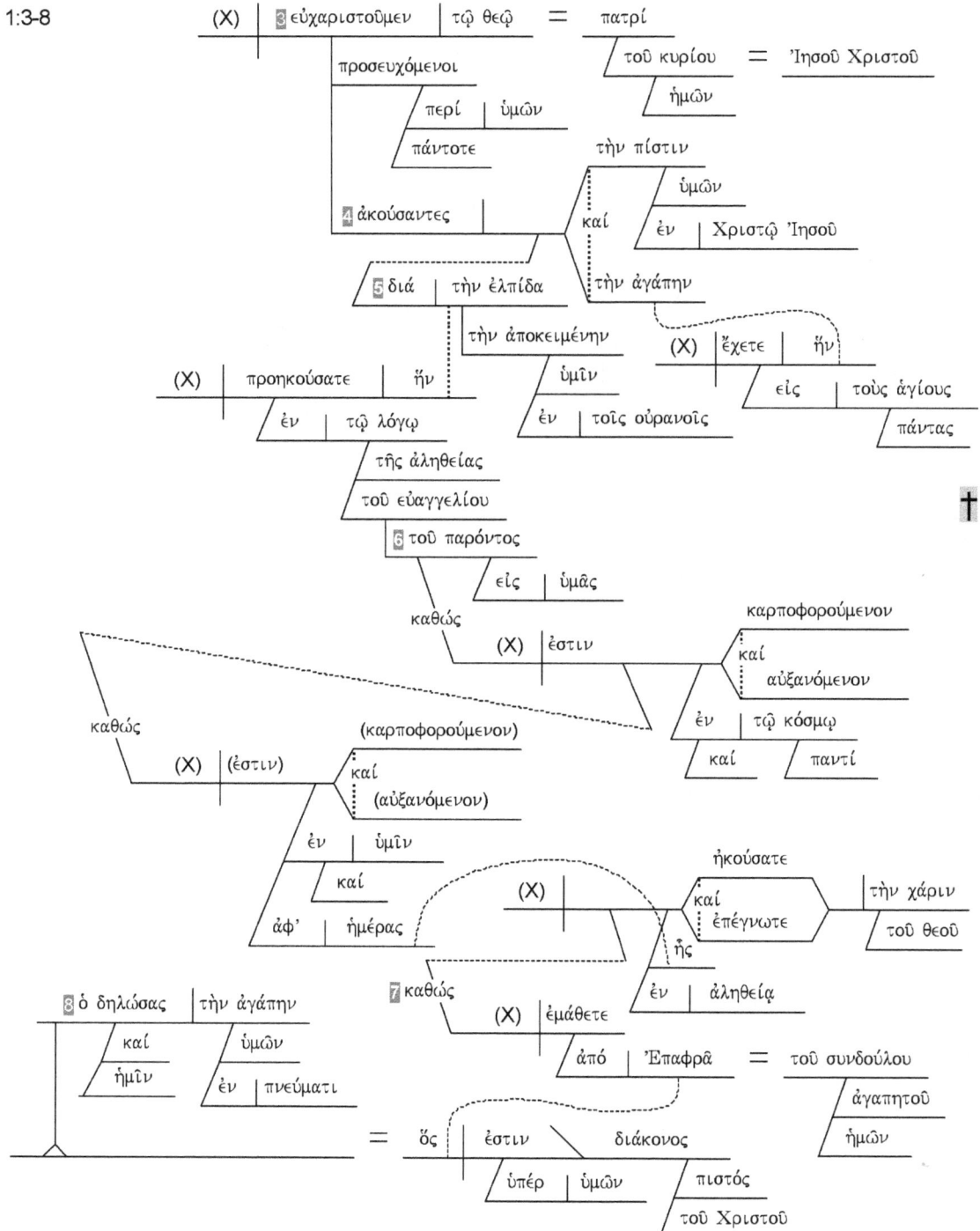

COLOSSIANS 1:9-15

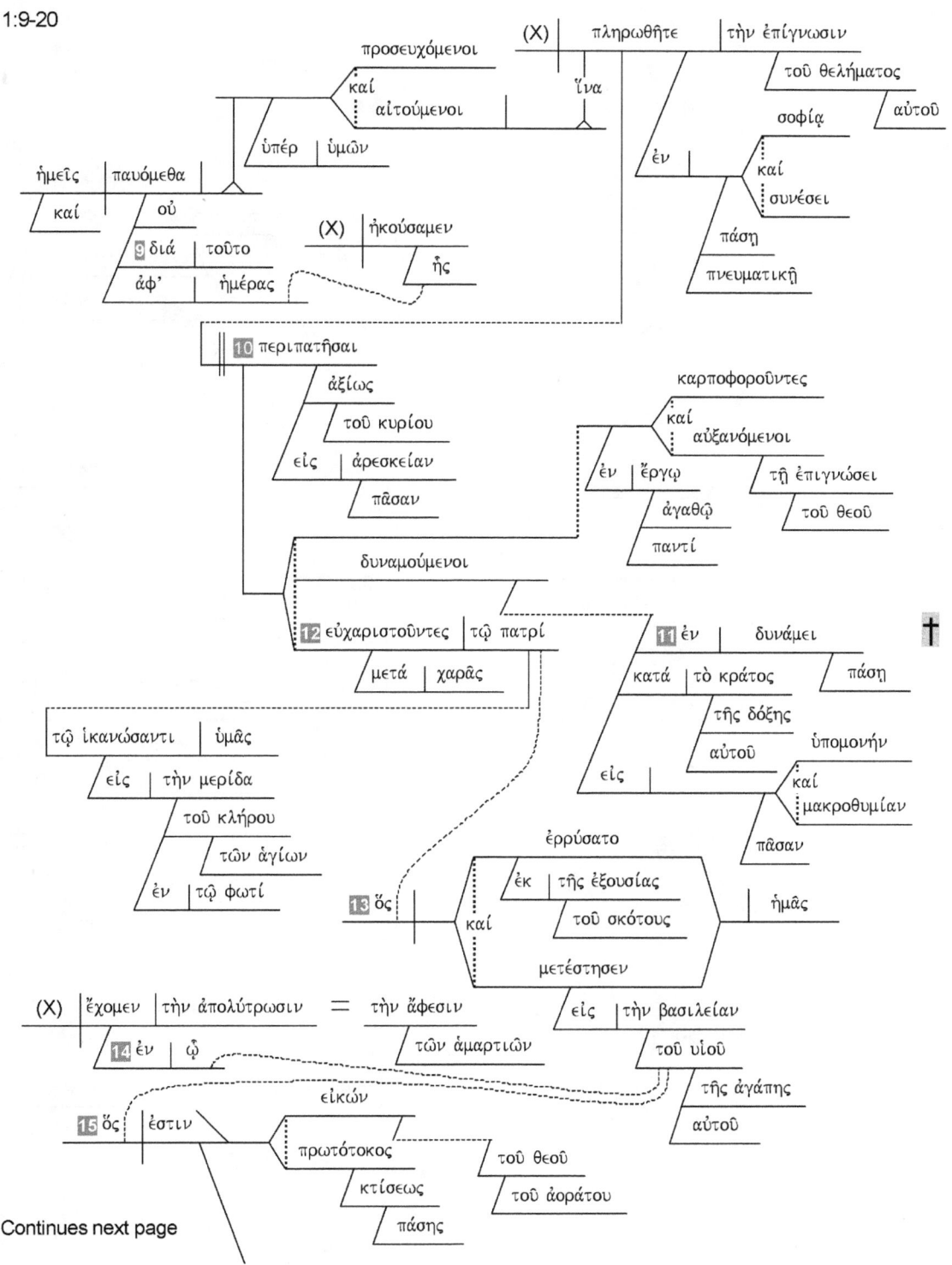

Continues next page

1:16-20 COLOSSIANS

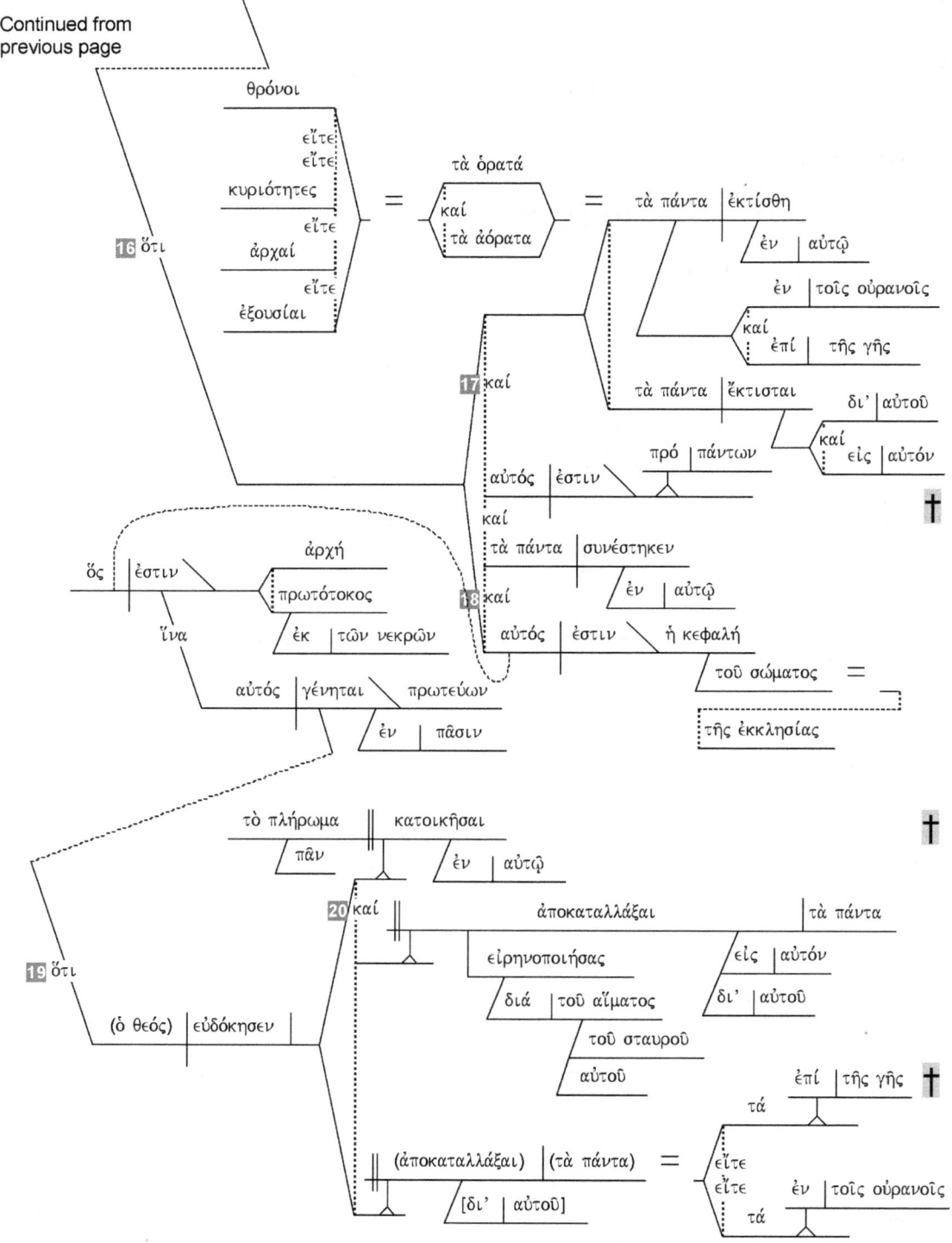

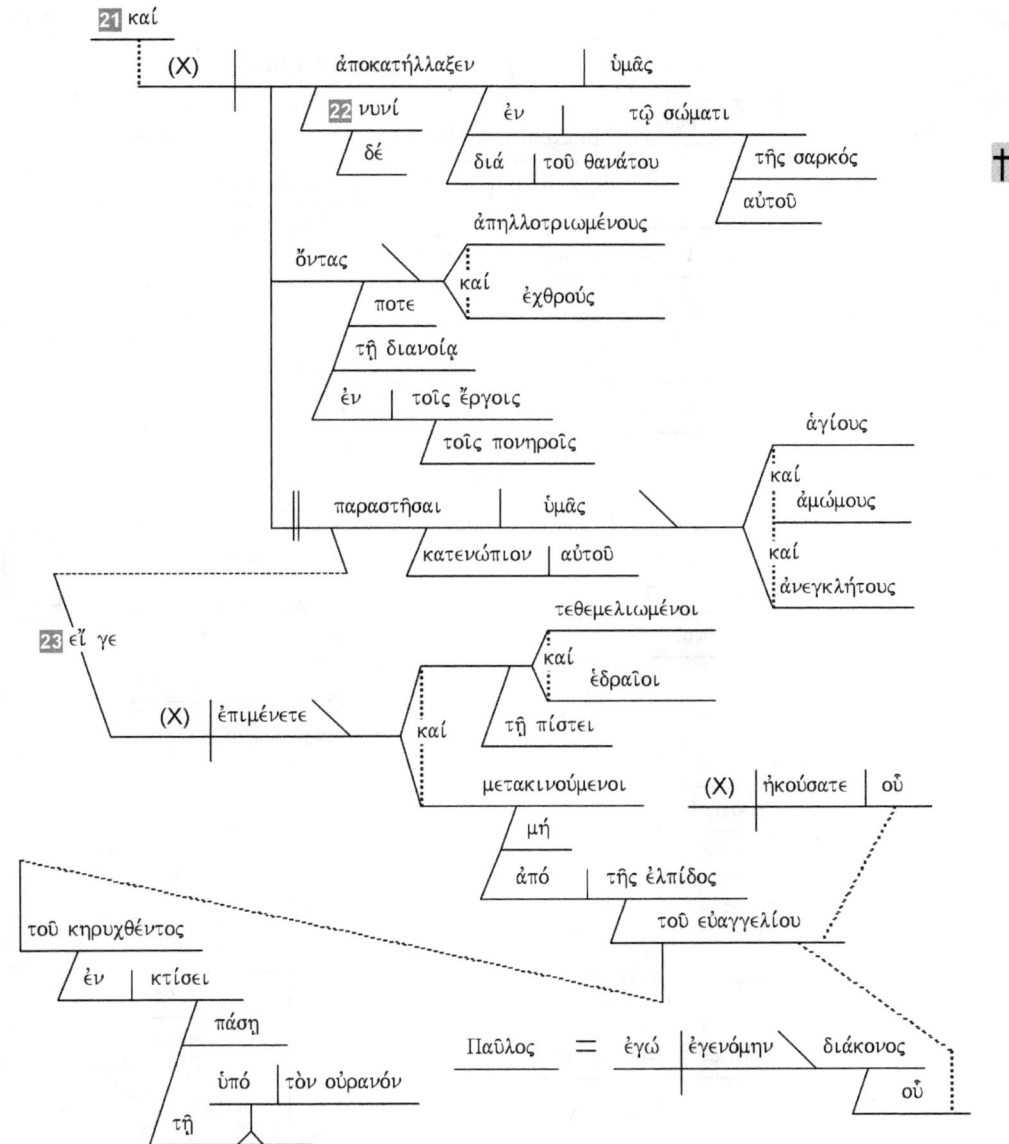

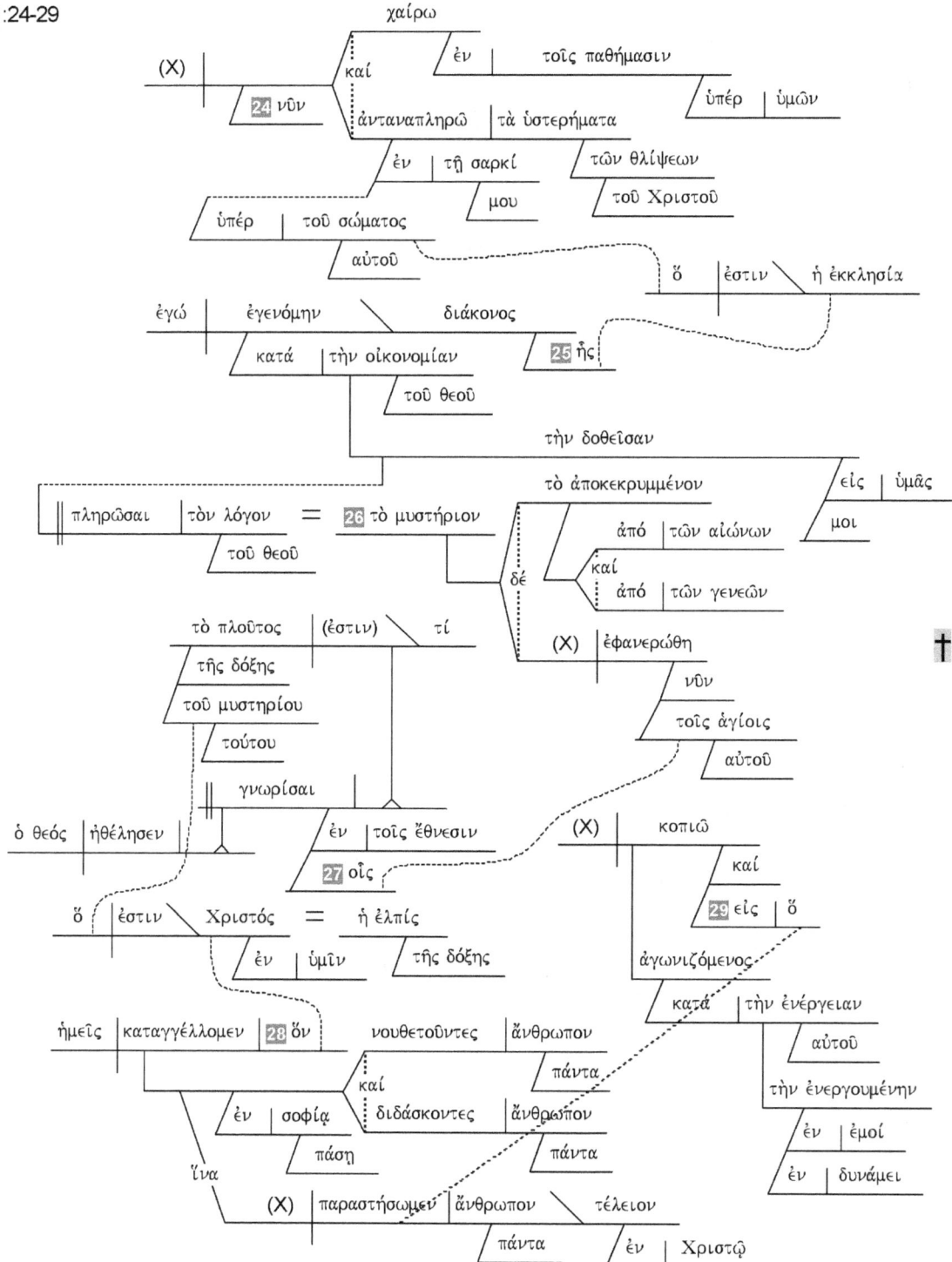

Notes on Colossians 1

Col 1:5 τοῦ εὐαγγελίου — The phrase could alternatively be construed as modifying ἀληθείας, but the parallel in Eph. 1:13, where εὐαγγέλιον can be understood only in apposition to λόγος, inclines me to construe those two together here as well.

Col 1:11 — I have ignored the period in v. 11, since what follows is an additional adverbial participle in the series.

Col 1:17 πρὸ πάντων — The phrase could alternatively be construed as adverbial to ἐστιν.

Col 1:19 πᾶν τὸ πλήρωμα — A number of versions take this phrase as a reference to the Godhead, eliminating the need for the admittedly awkward elliptical occurrence of "God" (or "the Father") as the subject of the verb. To me it seems slightly more awkward, however, to understand "all fulness" as an expression referring to God Himself. I am not aware of any parallel to such language, though certainly it is not impossible. I do not feel strongly about the preference reflected in the diagram; the passage is genuinely difficult.

Col 1:20 αὐτοῦ — Most of the versions construe this word with σταυροῦ ("his cross"). I have followed the NIV in construing it with αἵματος. One of the policies followed in these diagrams is, wherever natural, to reflect the Semitic pattern where, in an expression "X of Y of Z," in which Z is a personal pronoun, Z functions as a second modifier for X, not a modifier for Y. (E.g., "the word of the power of him" does not mean "the word of his power" but rather "his powerful word.") This particular example is unusual in that the Y term is ordinarily more abstract than "cross." The majority of versions may well be correct, but since the Semitic model does yield equally good sense, and since there is a clear example of it earlier in the sentence ("the son of his love" = "his beloved son"), I have adhered to the policy here also.

Col 1:22 δέ — It is hard to diagram this word. It is usually a coordinating conjunction, but there is no preceding finite verb to coordinate with the one it introduces (ἀποκατήλλαξεν). It does not coordinate this sentence with the preceding whole sentence; the opening καί in v. 21 serves that function. It seems clearly to mark a contrast between "now" in this clause and "formerly" in the opening participial section. Attempting to highlight that connection, I have diagrammed it as a modifier to "now."

Col 1:26 ἐφανερώθη — Semantically, this indicative verb is coordinate to the previous participle (ἀποκεκρυμμένον) and joined to it by δέ. Ordinarily one expects coordinate items to be grammatically as well as semantically parallel. The diagram here reflects the semantics rather than the grammar, which there does not seem to be a good way to reflect. Those with access to Grassmick's book will notice that he diagrammed it the same way as I did.

2:1-5 COLOSSIANS

2:1-3
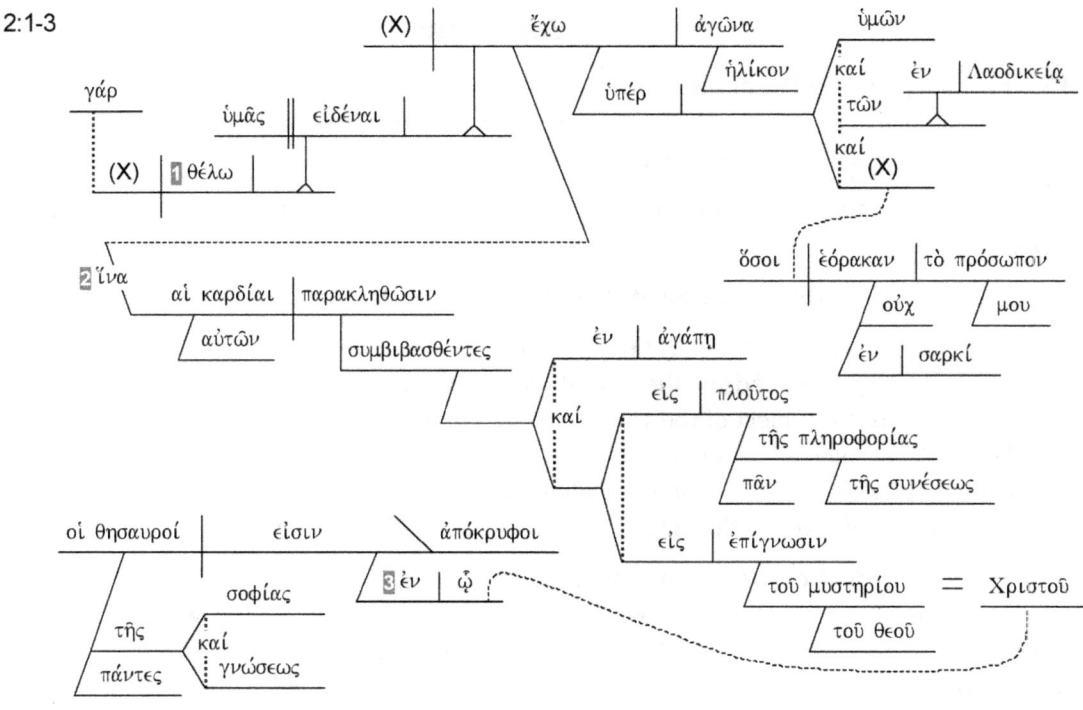

2:4
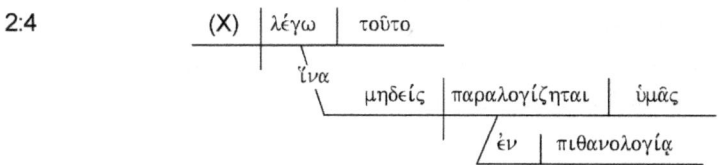

2:5
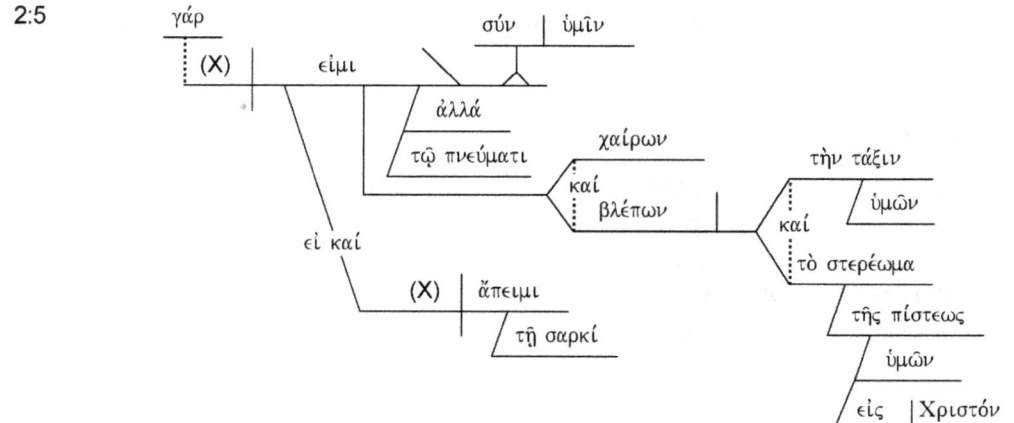

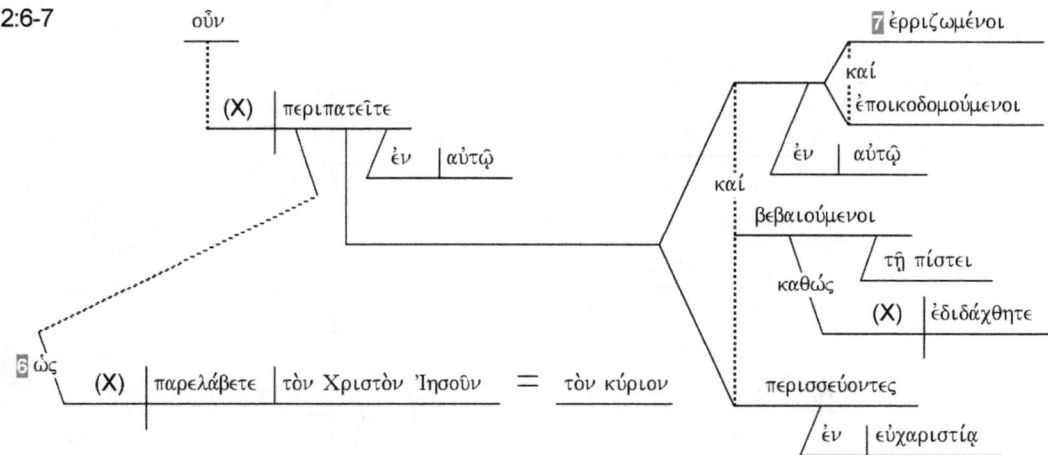

2:8-15

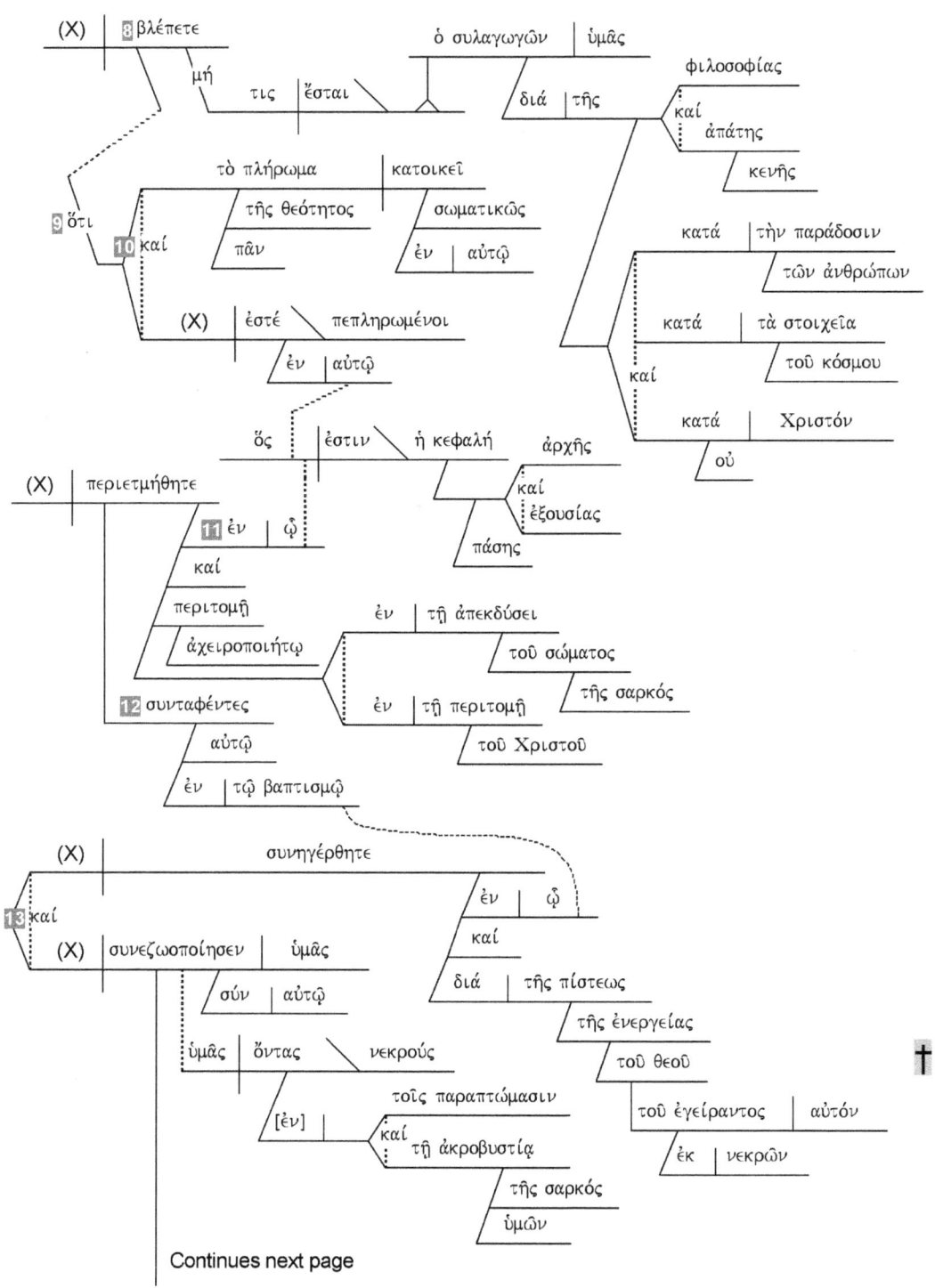

Continues next page

COLOSSIANS 2:14-17

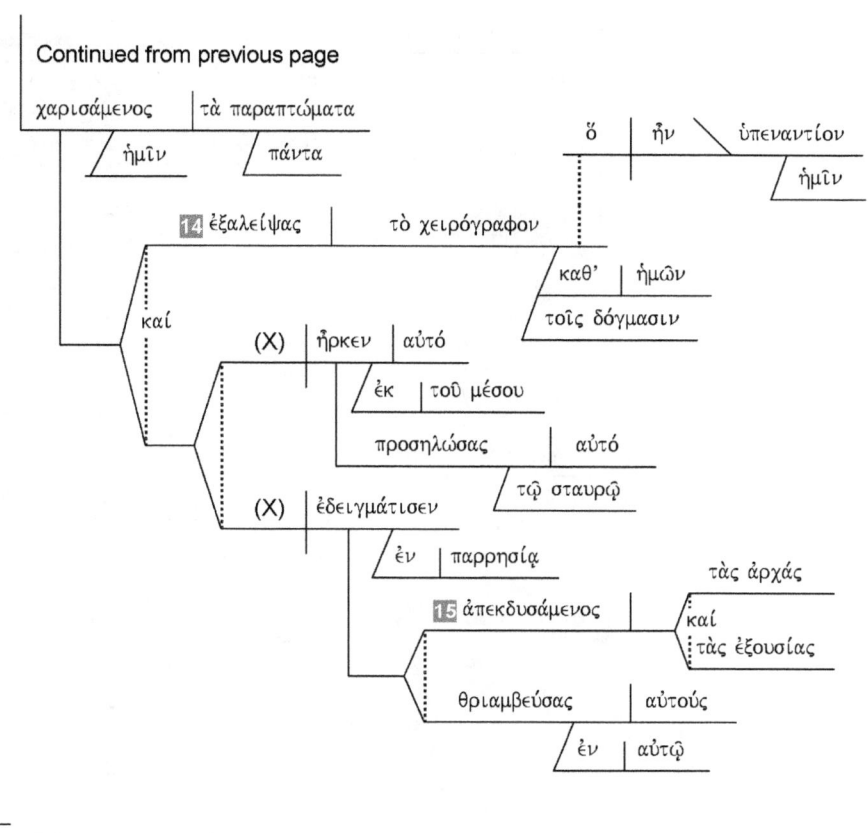

2:16-17

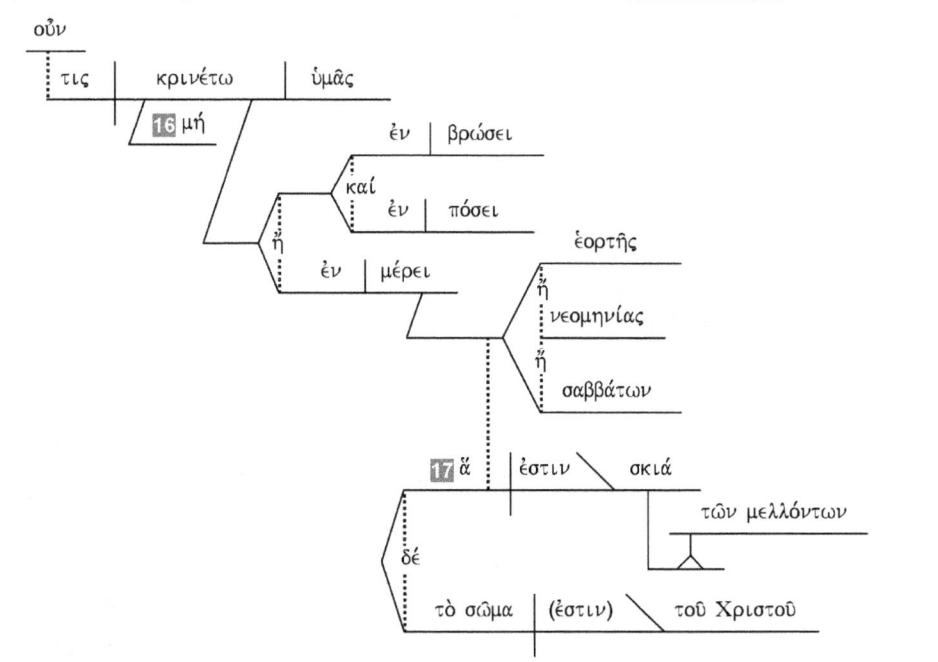

2:18-19

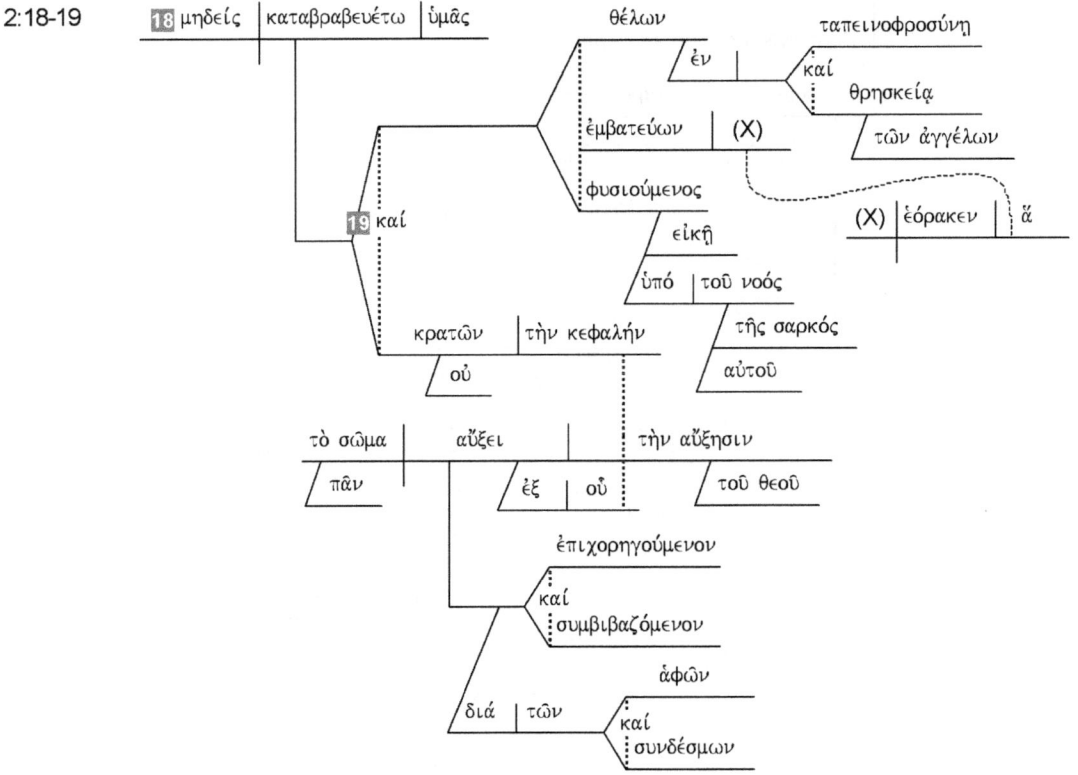

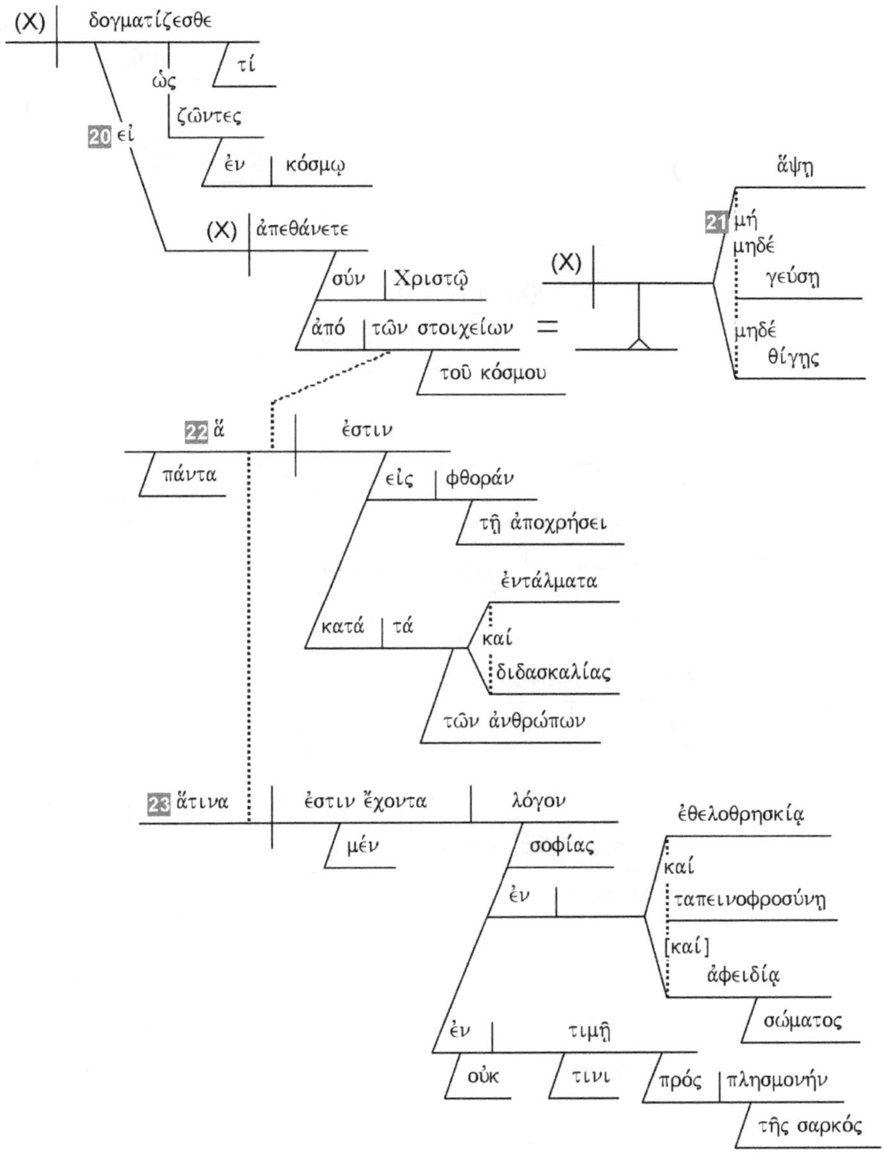

Notes on Colossians 2

Col 2:13 ὑμᾶς νεκροὺς ὄντας — I have diagrammed this as an accusative absolute. A case can be made that the construction is not absolute; it is accusative because the pronoun is conceived as the object of the verb συνεζωοποίησεν. The point is well taken, but there is a second pronoun serving as the object of that verb. If this word is also the object, then the language is redundant (which is, of course, quite possible). On that view, the best way I can think of to diagram would be to put both pronouns in the object slot and then diagram ὄντας as a simple adverbial participle.

3:1-4 COLOSSIANS

3:1-2

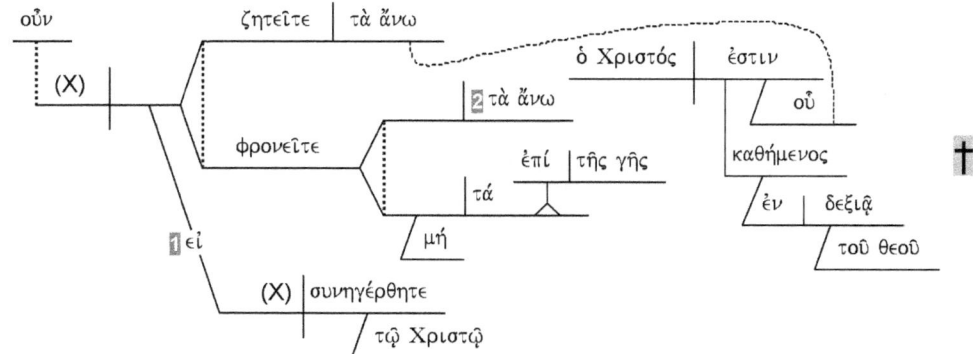

3:3-4

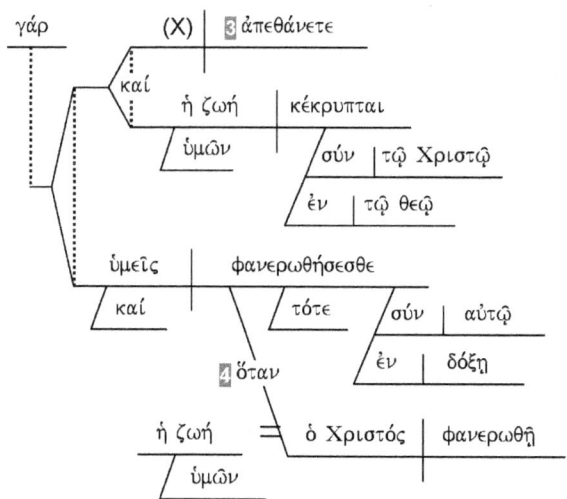

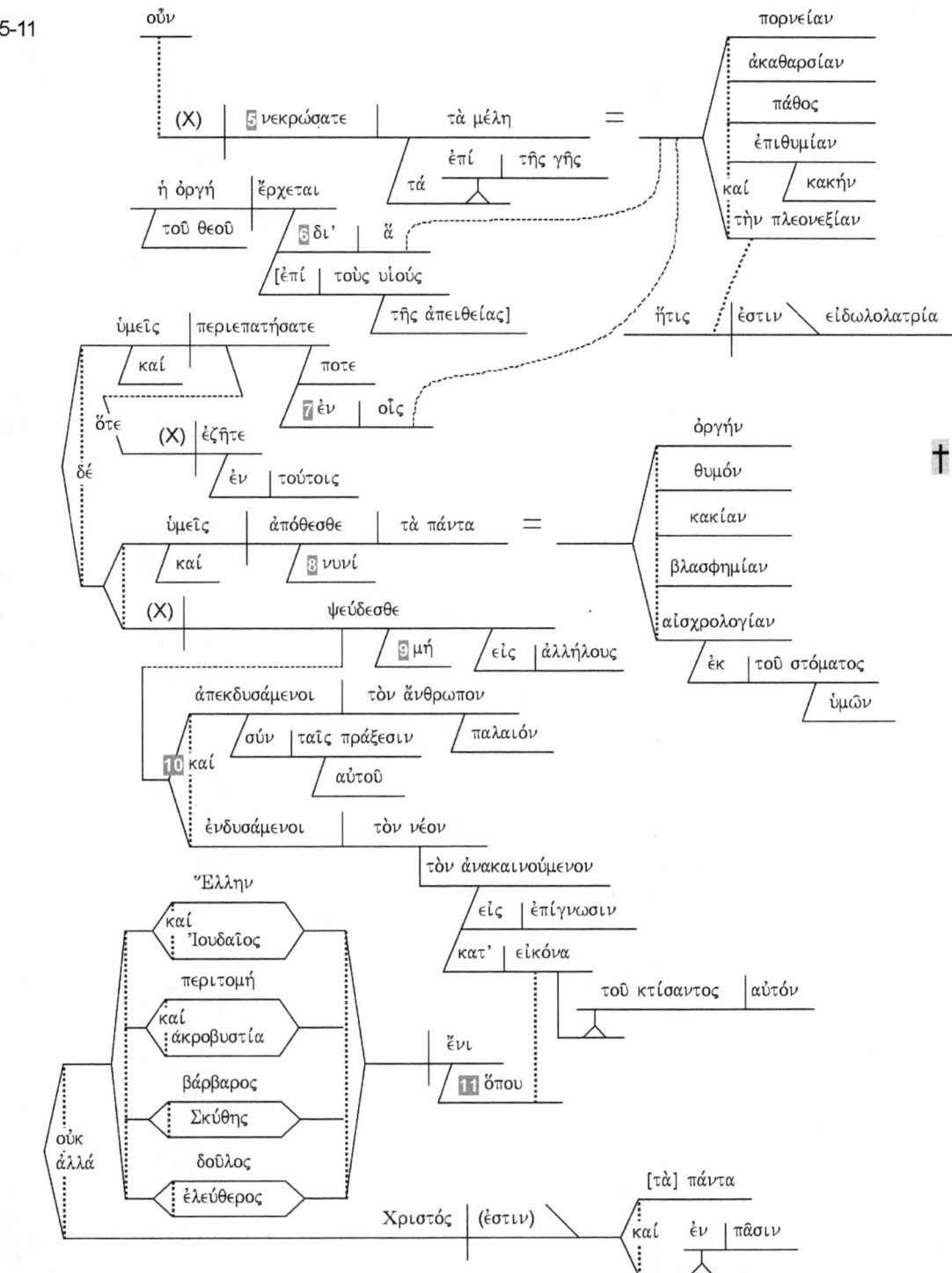

3:12-15 COLOSSIANS

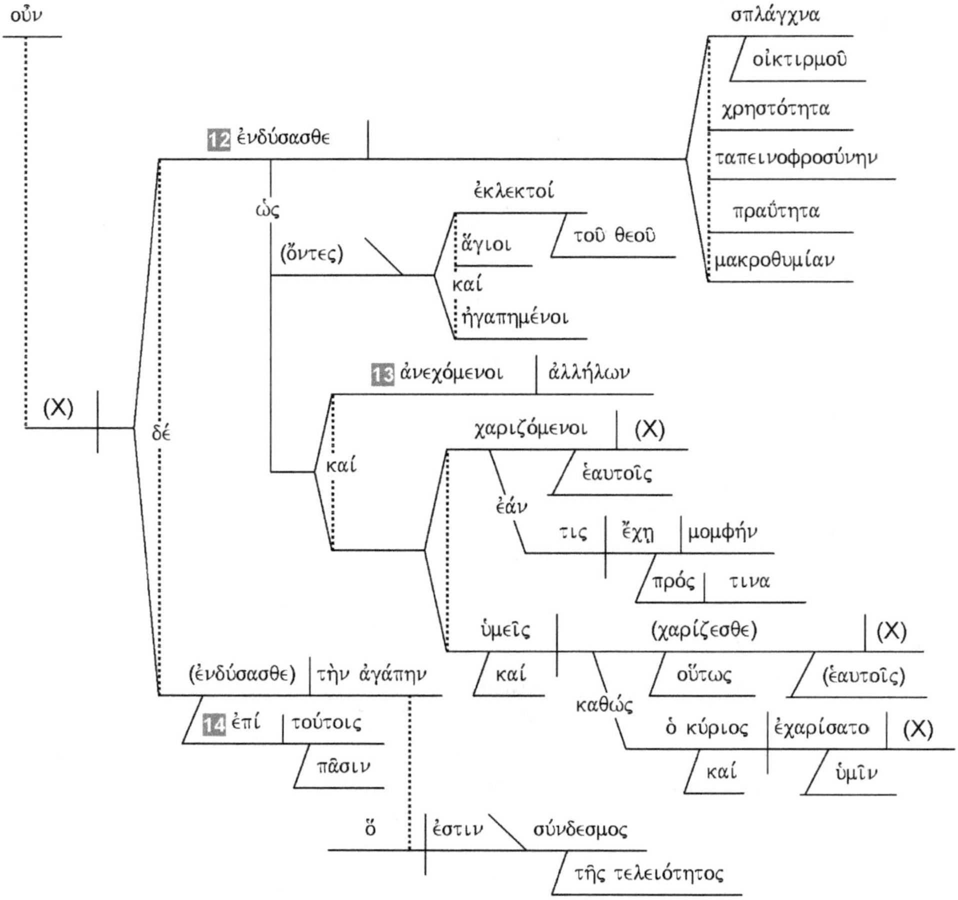

3:12-14

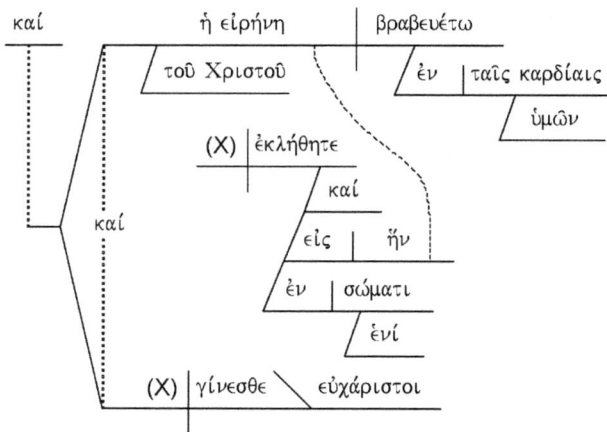

3:15

COLOSSIANS 3:16-19

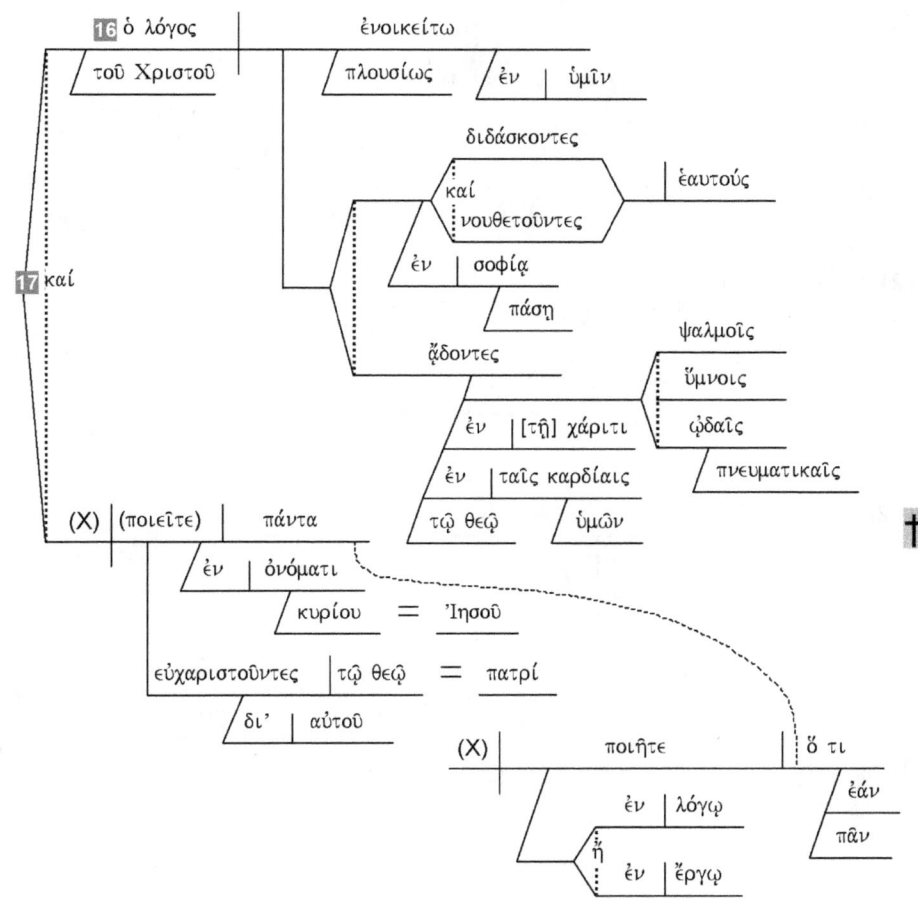

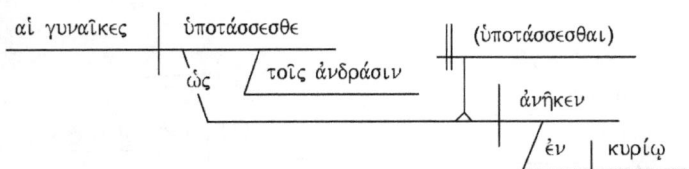

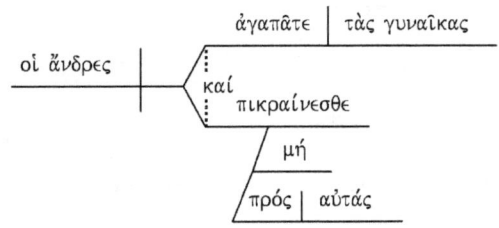

3:20-24a COLOSSIANS

3:20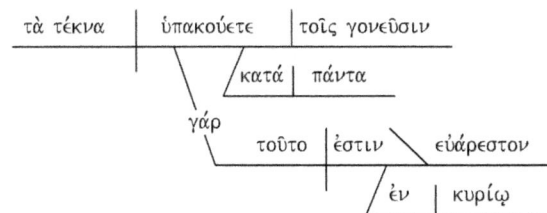

3:21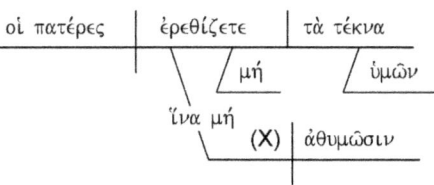

3:22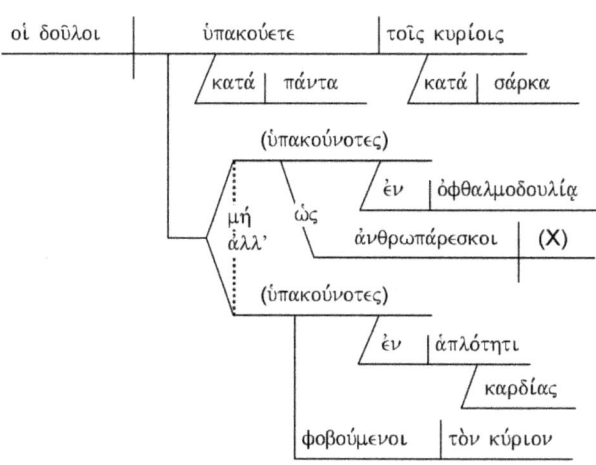

3:23-24a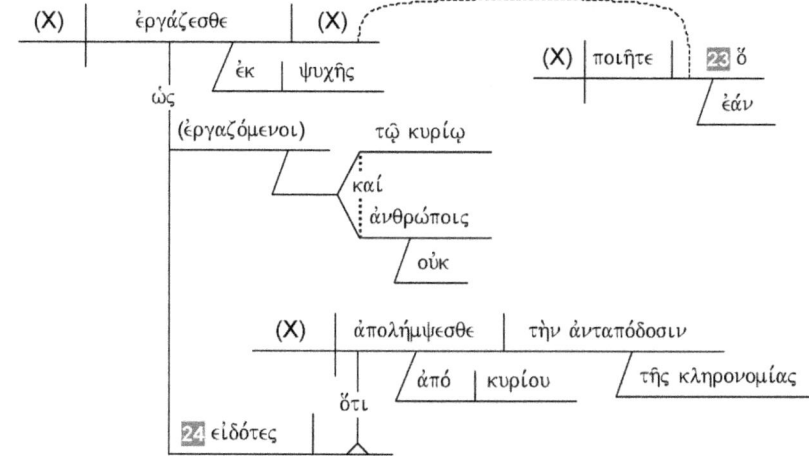

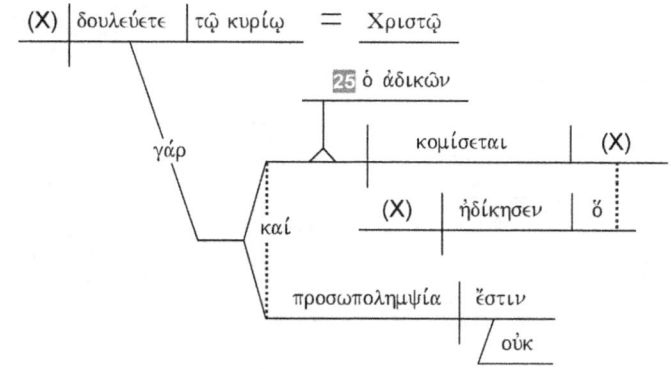

Notes on Colossians 3

Col 3:1 καθήμενος — The participle could alternatively be construed with ἐστιν as a periphrastic.

Col 3:7 οἷς, τούτοις — One of these pronouns could be taken as masculine, referring back to υἱούς in verse 6. My personal inclination is to do this with the relative pronoun, but I do not find any versions reading the passage so.

Col 3:16 τῷ θεῷ — The dative could alternatively be construed as modifying χάριτι.

Col 3:22 — The participle φοβούμενοι needs a verb form to govern it. The best construction I could think of to supply is a repetition of the verb, but in participle form (ὑπακούοντες), to avoid additional independent clauses. On this approach, an additional occurrence of the same participle is needed to balance the coordinate construction. The elliptical participles can be avoided if one is willing to diagram φοβούμενοι as a modifier connected somewhere in the "in sincerity of heart" clause.

COLOSSIANS

4:1-5

4:1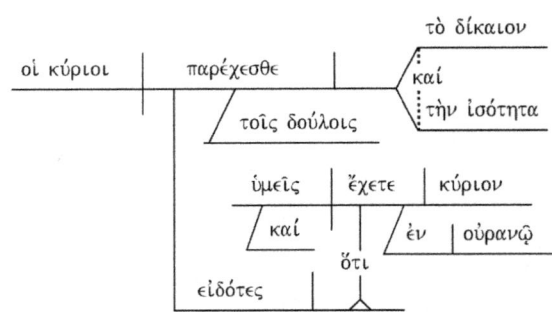

4:2-4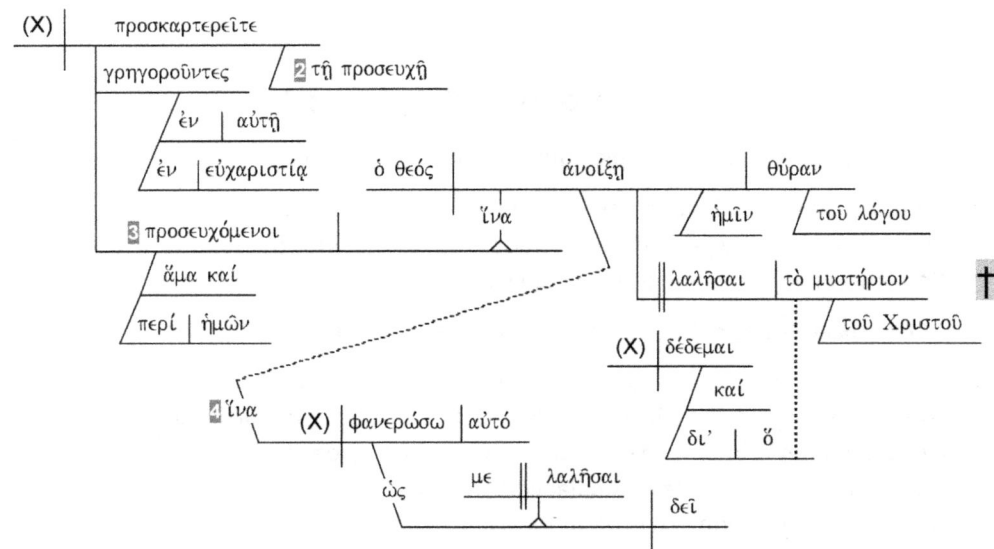

4:5

4:6

ἐν
χάριτι
ὁ λόγος
(ἔστω)
ὑμῶν
πάντοτε
ἠρτυμένος
ἅλατι
ὑμᾶς
ἀποκρίνεσθαι
δεῖ
πῶς
ἑνί
εἰδέναι
ἑκάστῳ

4:7-9

ἀδελφός
ἀγαπητός
καί
ὁ
διάκονος
πιστός
καί
σύνδουλος
ἐν
κυρίῳ
Τύχικος
γνωρίσει
7 τά
κατ'
ἐμέ
ὑμῖν
πάντα
(X)
ἔπεμψα
8 ὅν
πρός
ὑμᾶς
εἰς
τοῦτο
αὐτό
9 σύν
Ὀνησίμῳ
τῷ ἀδελφῷ
πιστῷ
καί
ἀγαπητῷ
ὅς
ἐστιν
ἐξ
ὑμῶν
ἵνα
περί
ἡμῶν
(X)
γνῶτε
τά
καί
(X)
παρακαλέσῃ
τὰς καρδίας
ὑμῶν
(X)
γνωρίσουσιν
τὰ ὧδε
ὑμῖν
πάντα

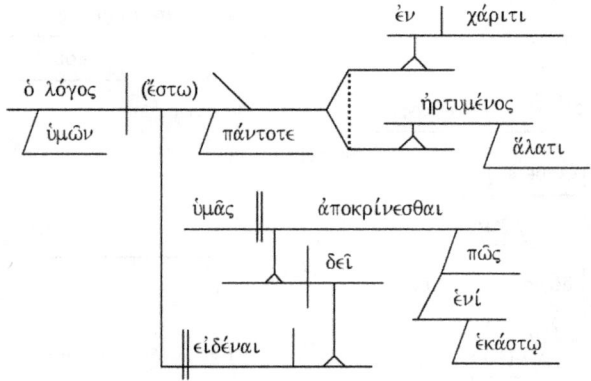

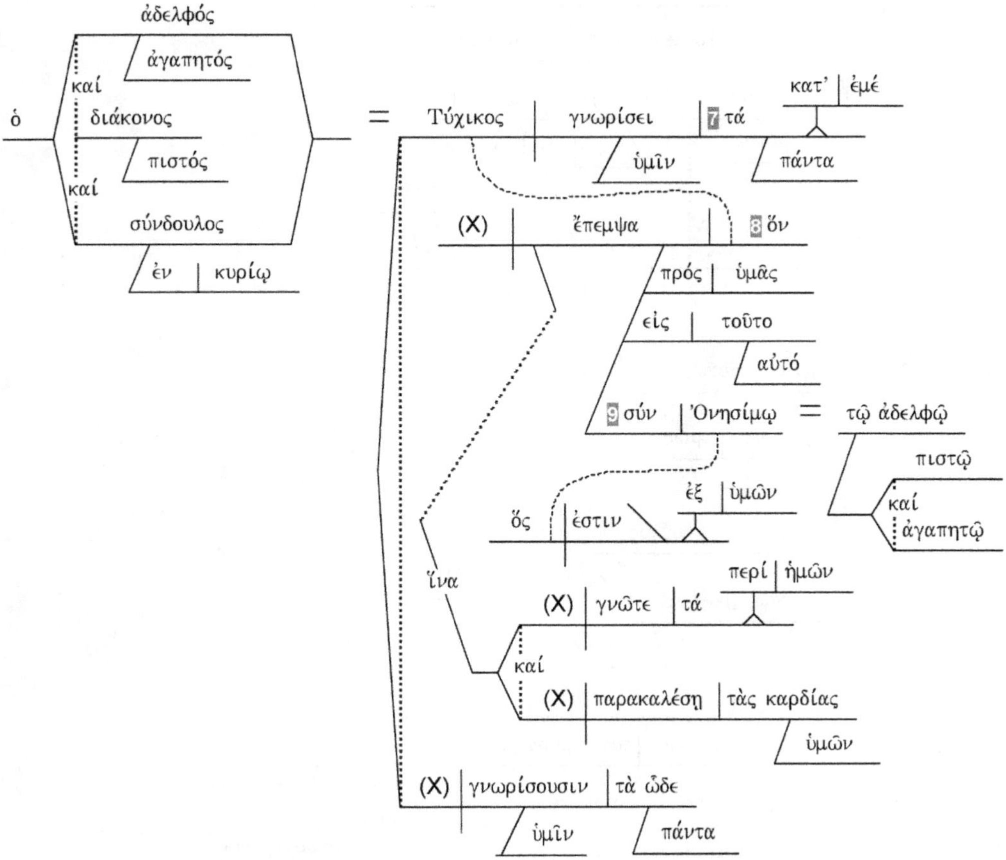

4:10-12 COLOSSIANS

4:10-11

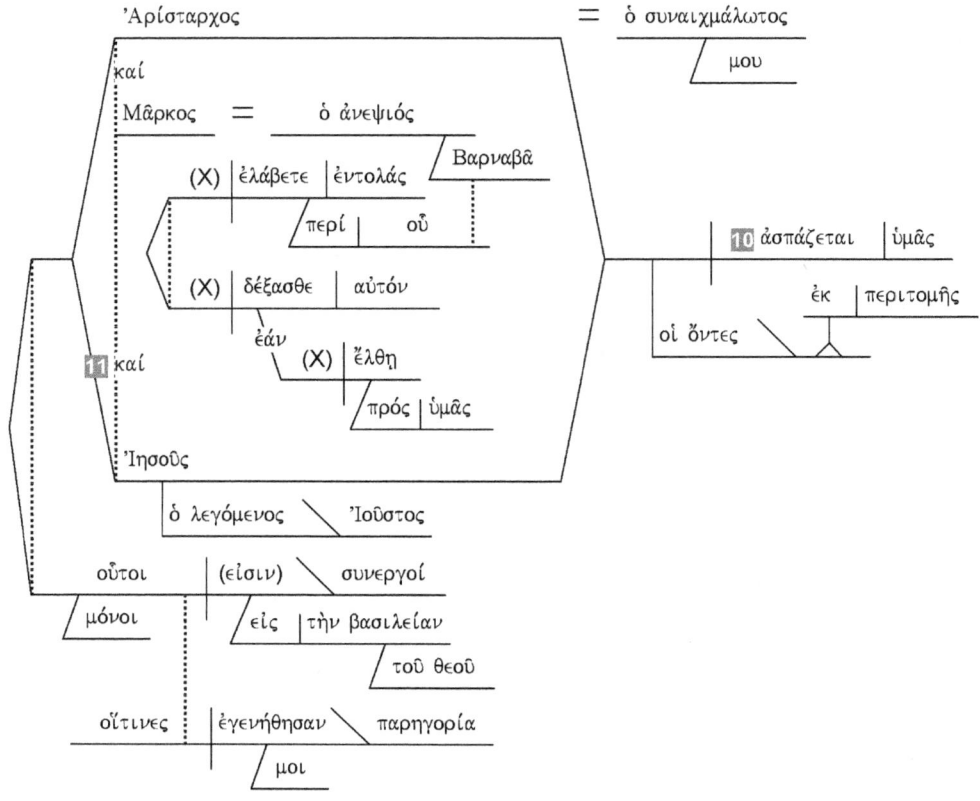

4:12

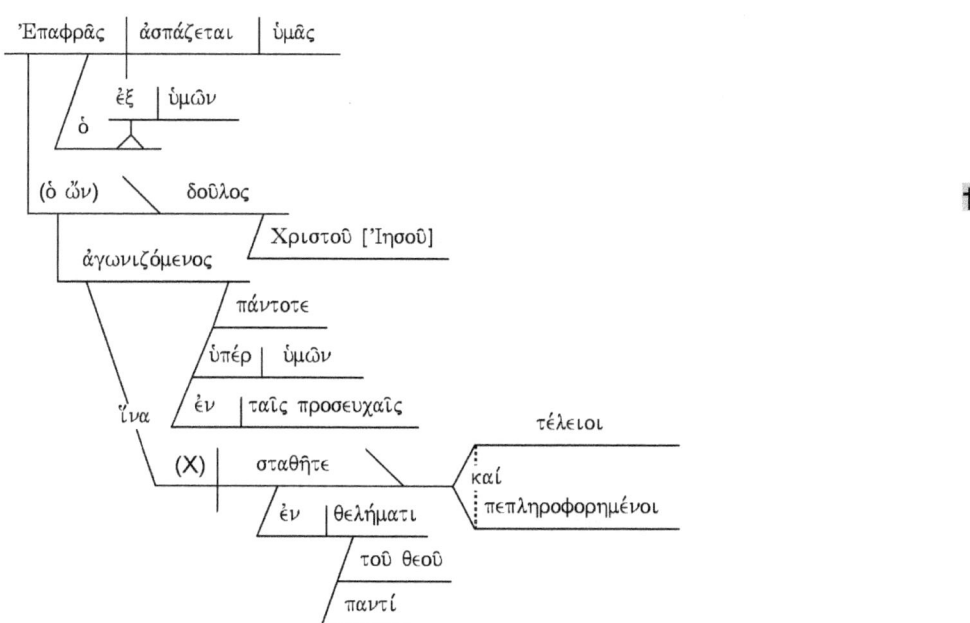

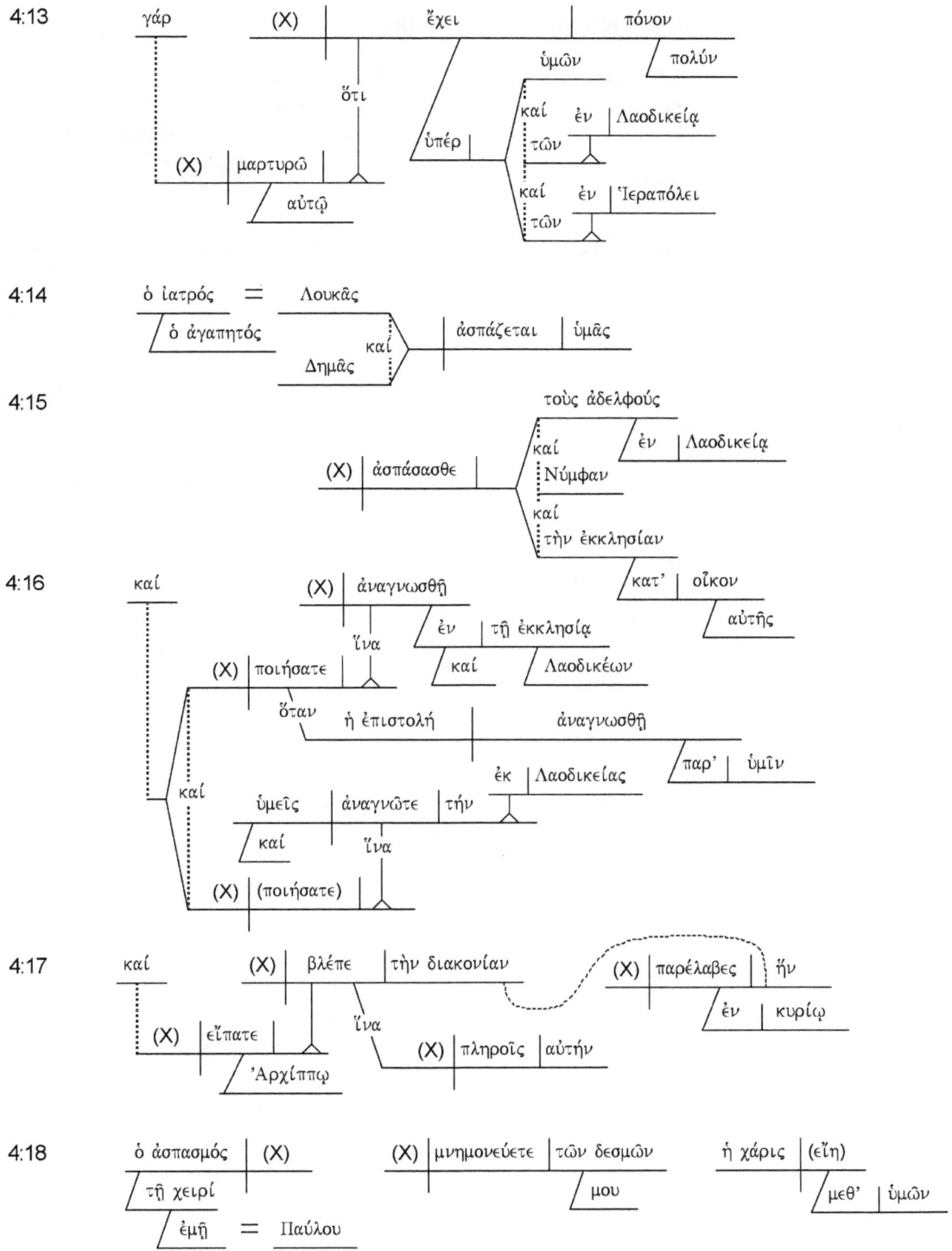

Notes on Colossians 4

Col 4:3 ἅμα καί — BDAG appears to treat this expression as an adverbial unit.

Col 4:12 (ὁ ὤν) — I have supplied this attributive participle in order to have a verb form to govern the adverbial participle ἀγωνιζόμενος. The thought connection I see is that the participle supplies either the evidence that, the degree to which, or the respect in which Epaphras is a servant of Christ. These are adverbial thought connections, not adjectival or nominal ones that would justify diagramming ἀγωνιζόμενος more simply as attributive or appositional to δοῦλος.

Col 4:17 — The ἵνα clause could also be diagrammed as a second object of βλέπε, coordinate to τὴν διακονίαν. I have diagrammed it as a purpose clause.

New Testament Greek Sentence Diagramming

by Randy Leedy   This article is reproduced from Biblical Viewpoint 39, no. 1 (April 2005):17-39. Released to the public domain, 2020, with a request that all further publication include this statement of origin.

Making a Case for Sentence Diagramming

For many people the expression *sentence diagramming* evokes painful memories of Junior High English class. At the time, at least, it seemed like a perfectly mysterious thing: doing it correctly, or at least to the teacher's satisfaction, seemed utterly impossible, and equally impossible was envisioning any useful purpose it could possibly serve. But all of that was before we discovered the value of New Testament Greek exegesis. Many of us learned the mechanics of Greek grammar without drawing any sentence diagrams. It did not occur to most of us that what we were learning was equipping us to draw diagrams quite skillfully if we had wanted to do so. We were learning, for example, how to pick out the subject and predicate of the sentence, how to determine that a certain adjective modifies a certain noun, whether a participle functions as an adjective, a noun, or an adverb, and whether an infinitive functions as subject, complement, or adverbially. We learned to tell the difference between prepositions and conjunctions, and we learned how to find each preposition's object, whether that object be a noun, pronoun, or infinitive. We learned to tease apart a complex sentence's various clauses, distinguishing between the main and subordinate clauses. We learned how relative clauses work: that the whole clause has an adjectival function modifying some other part of the sentence and that the relative pronoun has a noun function within the clause it introduces. We learned that some conjunctions signal grammatical parallelism and that others indicate subordinate relationships.

Perhaps most importantly we learned the value of this sort of information. We learned that, by carefully sorting out the mechanics of the sentence according to the language's grammatical rules we could eventually discover the meaning of sentences that initially mystified us.[1] We learned that, apart from

---

[1] Often, of course, we found ourselves facing more than one possibility of interpretation. Usually one interpretation would commend itself to us as best, but sometimes we were left uncertain. Neverthe-

our understanding of grammatical mechanics, we would be left with no option but to make wild guesses at meaning according to some impressionistic sense of what those words seemed to say. We realized that this is exactly how we interpreted our native language: according to impressionistic sense rather than strict grammar. However, we realized that we have such an instinctive feel for our native language's grammar that our impressions of meaning are for the most part quite accurate. So learning to diagram sentences in our own language seemed pointless: our diagram told us nothing more about meaning than what we knew perfectly well before we began. We also learned, however, that the situation is considerably different in the study of the Biblical texts. The original languages are not our native language. The translations we read in our native language are not always able to reproduce precisely the grammatical structures of the original. The meaning we derive from even a skilled reading of a skillful translation is not always exactly the same meaning we derive from careful exegesis of the Greek text. We learned the significance of that little expression *careful exegesis*. We learned that we could give a cursory glance to the Greek text without finding anything beyond what we saw in our English version, but that more careful attention to the Greek often uncovered details of meaning that otherwise we would have missed. By hearing our teachers point out and explain details that in fact we *had* missed, we learned that the ideal exegetical mindset is intent upon examining every detail of wording in search of meaning.[2]

Once we come to understand the value of ransacking a text for potentially significant details, one of the mysteries of sentence diagramming evaporates: we now see clearly a valuable purpose. One kind of exegetical detail that we want to be sure to explore thoroughly is the matter of the basic connections between words, phrases, and clauses within a sentence. Dragging our eyes across the sentence is not a sufficiently disciplined approach to this particular exegetical task. Forcing ourselves to account for these details on paper is an approach that holds much greater promise of keeping us from missing things. Many of us learned this sort of discipline by producing detailed parsing sheets in our exegesis classes. We thought about every word in the passage at least long

---

less, uncertainty among several possible meanings is infinitely better than being left at a complete loss to give even one clear interpretation.

[2] Of course we also had to learn that *not* every detail can be pressed safely. We learned, for example, that many prepositions share the same meaning, that possible distinctions between synonyms cannot always be maintained, and that the presence or absence of the definite article cannot always be insisted upon as exegetically significant. In all this we learned that we face a lifetime of growth in our exegetical acumen as we develop increasing sensitivity not only to what significance grammatical details *may* have but what significance a given context will support that grammatical details actually *do* have in that case.

enough to decide whether or not it presented us with questions or difficulties regarding its form or its usage category that we wanted to record on paper for future reference.

Sentence diagramming is another such exegesis tool that forces us to deal with every word in the sentence, this time with the goal of mapping out the sentence schematically in order to develop confidence that our understanding of the sentence's basic skeleton is correct. That word *confidence* is an important one. As preachers and teachers of the Word, we need confidence that we understand it accurately. Where does that confidence come from? There is a subjective dimension to that confidence, in which the Spirit of God operates within us to assure us that we are speaking the truth. God has also provided an objective basis for confidence, however, in the very nature of language and history. The grammatical-historical approach to interpretation provides means of testing the validity of our interpretation. Is our interpretation consistent with the meanings that the words and grammatical structures can be demonstrated regularly to have? Is our interpretation consistent with relevant historical facts as best we understand them? Sentence diagramming is a very powerful tool within the grammatical prong of that hermeneutical approach to scripture in that it enables us to demonstrate to ourselves that we are taking the individual words of the sentence consistently with the language's regular grammatical principles. Apart from a relatively complete understanding of a sentence's grammatical mechanics, we have no objective basis for confidence that our understanding of the sentence's meaning is correct.

Sometimes we are overconfident in our interpretation. I like to illustrate this fact with a line from a beloved hymn, "Be Thou My Vision." The hymn begins, "Be Thou my vision, O Lord of my heart; Naught be all else to me save that Thou art." I often ask students to paraphrase that second part. Some are pretty much at a loss: they have an impression that they can't quite put into words. Others do get something into words, and they typically do well with the meanings of the words *naught* and *save*, invariably suggesting something like "May I value nothing but You." They are always quite confident that their interpretation is correct. But they have trouble, when pressed, to explain why the poet wrote "that Thou art" rather than simply "Thou." The best they can do is to suggest that more syllables were needed to fill out the poetic meter. But a good poet doesn't waste syllables, and this is good poetry. Is there a difference in meaning between "that Thou art" (i.e., "what you are") and "Thou"? Obviously, yes. Recasting the poetic line in modern prose would yield something like this: "May everything except what You are be nothing to me." The subject is "all else" (expanded by "save that Thou art"), the verb is "be," and the complement is "naught." The phrase "to me" means "in my estimation"; it is probably adverbial. So the topic (subject) of the clause is "all else save that Thou art" or "everything except what You are," and the predicate is "may [it, the subject] be in my estimation nothing." This yields a different meaning than "May nothing but You be anything to me." What is Christ? Well, for example, He is "wisdom, and righteousness, and sanctification, and redemption" (I Cor. 1:30). So those are things the poet does want to value, because the pursuit of those things will lead him to the Christ who is those things. This line of exegesis proves very fruitful. The extra detail of meaning was not such as to completely overturn our initial understanding, but it certainly sharpens it up and expands it. Suppose we were content with the thought "May nothing but Christ be anything to me," in the sense that I want to pursue nothing in life but Christ. OK, I'll start pursuing Christ. But what direction will I turn? Where do I think He is? How will I know when I have found Him? Am I expecting to find him in a building or under a rock or on a mountain or beside a tree? Will I recognize Him by face? It is hard to know how to pursue Christ, but it is not so hard to know how to pursue the things God reveals that Christ is. God's Word tells me how to pursue wisdom, righteousness, etc., and now I can put specific shape and direction to my pursuit of Christ.

After attending carefully to the grammatical structure of the English sentence they are interpreting, my students find that their initial confidence was somewhat unwarranted. Were they content with their initial impression, they would be on basically the right track, but they would miss the clarity of understanding that exegetical care produces. After a few experiences of this sort with a variety of literature, one begins to get the idea that there must be many places in Scripture where exegetical care can produce new confidence about meaning previously understood or reveal new details about meaning never before noticed. Such a one can be sure that his exegetical labors, if well founded grammatically and historically, will not go unrewarded. And a sentence's basic mapping, as displayed in a sentence diagram, is one dimension of that exegetical labor that deserves all the detailed attention one is able to devote to it.

Skilled Greek exegetes may find that the actual diagramming exercise does not bring much benefit, because their minds are trained to attend to those details without the extra labor of drawing them out on paper. Would-be exegetes seriously lacking grammatical acumen may likewise find little benefit in diagramming, as they sense that they are simply drawing out a map regarding which they have neither any confidence nor any basis for evaluation and correction. I would like to suggest, though, that in addition to being a valuable exercise for the developing exegete with a good degree of grammatical mastery, diagramming may perhaps serve as a basis for bringing together pedagogically the polar extremes. The skilled exegetes, in the classroom or in their writing, could help the unskilled develop greater skills by showing their understanding diagrammatically in addition to explaining it in technical prose. Couple this potential value with the fact that there appears to be an increasing interest in sentence diagramming among Greek exegetes, teachers, and students, and there is adequate reason to pursue mastery of some relatively standard method of diagramming grammatical relationships within sentences. Several handbooks on diagramming are available,[3] several advanced Bible software packages include diagramming tools,[4] (the diagrams in this article were drawn with BibleWorks version 6.0) and at least one complete set of NT sentence diagrams is available.[5]

The purpose of this article is to set out some basic diagramming conventions, make some suggestions about the degree of detail most productively codified in those conventions, and encourage wider use of sentence diagramming in the exegesis and teaching of NT Greek. I hope it may prove possible in this way to remove the other mystery of our Junior High days, which was how to draw the diagrams satisfactorily. Though the article will explain a few basic points of grammar, for the most part I assume that the reader has a solid understanding of such matters as parts of speech and major sentence elements such as clauses (dependent and independent, made up of subject, verb, and various kinds of complements) prepositional phrases, modifiers, and conjunctions. A reader who fears his understanding of these points is weak is encouraged to give the article a try. He may well find that he is better equipped for it than he thought.

Some cautions are in order, though. First, one should not think that a sentence diagram represents an exhaustive account of every relevant grammatical detail. Diagramming shows basic grammatical connections, but not every

---

[3] I am aware of two works completely devoted to sentence diagramming: Lee Kantenwein, *Diagrammatical Analysis* (Winona Lake, Ind.: BMH Books, 1979) and Richard P. Belcher, *Diagramming the Greek NT* (Columbia, SC: Richbarry Press, 1985). As far as I know the Belcher title is out of print. Two other more general works on exegesis contain substantial sections dealing with sentence diagramming: John D. Grassmick, *Principles and Practice of Greek Exegesis* (Dallas: Dallas Theological Seminary, 1976) and Thomas Schreiner, *Interpreting the Pauline Epistles* (Grand Rapids: Baker, 1990).

[4] BibleWorks and Logos/Libronix (for Windows) and Accordance (for Macintosh) are the ones I am aware of.

[5] Gerhard Raske, *The Grammatical Blueprint Bible*. For information see http://www.kwic.com/~graske/. BibleWorks is also in the process of producing a complete set of NT diagrams. The epistles are currently slated for release in Fall of 2005.

relevant detail. For example, a genitive-case noun will be diagrammed as modifying its head word, but there remains a wide range of possibilities regarding the exact thought connection between the two. So, for example, the expression "righteousness of God" will be diagrammed to show that "of God" modifies "righteousness," but the diagram will not show whether the exact meaning is "a believer's righteousness that comes from God" or "God's own righteousness." Nor will it show anything about word meaning: a diagram cannot show whether *righteousness* signifies actual righteous character and/or conduct or a righteous standing before God's Law. Furthermore, sentence diagramming deals only with grammatical relationships among words, phrases, and clauses within individual sentences. It is powerless to show the logical development of thought across larger units of text. Other methods of diagramming are needed for that purpose. But since individual words are the most useful basic building blocks of sentences,[6] sentence diagramming is foundational to any other sort of diagramming with the larger units of thought.

Conventions for Sentence Diagramming

Like machines or human bodies, complex sentences do not consist of a single amorphous mass. They break down into grammatical parts, each of which breaks down further into smaller parts. The largest unit within a sentence is the clause, which consists of a subject (the topic under discussion) and a predicate (the statement made about the topic, or in the case of an interrogative sentence, the question asked about the topic). The words making up a clause may be divided into kernel elements, modifiers, and introductory words. We will take up these categories in order.

Diagramming Kernel Elements

The kernel elements are those expressing the core of the subject and predicate: the subject is the noun or pronoun naming the clause's topic, and the predicate consists minimally of the verb, though many if not most verbs also demand a complement (such as a direct object or a predicate nominative). The kernel elements then, are subject, verb, and, if required, complement. The most

---

[6] I say "most useful" in order to indicate practicality and the average person's perception. Individual words are not the smallest building blocks; they consist of yet smaller elements, the roots and combining forms that have definable meanings. But the fact that we separate words on the page with spaces shows that we are especially conscious of them as the basic pieces of meaning with which we work to express ourselves.

reliable way to locate the kernel is to find the verb and express it in its proper voice, then ask "who or what?" *before* the verb to find its subject, then ask "who(m) or what?" *after* the verb to find any complement. A verb that does not require a complement will not lend itself to the complement question.

We will use a single sentence from the Greek New Testament as an example for a substantial portion of our discussion. John 12:16 reads as follows: ταῦτα οὐκ ἔγνωσαν αὐτοῦ οἱ μαθηταὶ τὸ πρῶτον, ἀλλ᾽ ὅτε ἐδοξάσθη Ἰησοῦς τότε ἐμνήσθησαν ὅτι ταῦτα ἦν ἐπ᾽ αὐτῷ γεγραμμένα καὶ ταῦτα ἐποίησαν αὐτῷ ("These things his disciples did not know at the first, but when Jesus was glorified, then they remembered that these things had been written about him and these things they did to him.") The main clause of this sentence is ταῦτα οὐκ ἔγνωσαν αὐτοῦ οἱ μαθηταὶ τὸ πρῶτον — "the disciples did not know these things at first."[7] The verb is ἔγνωσαν, which signifies knowing and is active voice. We may find the subject by asking, "Who or what knows?" (Notice that the phrasing of the verb is very simple. It is important to reflect the active voice, but at this point there is no need for concern over details such as tense or the fact that the verb is negated by οὐκ.) The whole subject phrase is αὐτοῦ οἱ μαθηταί ("his disciples"). But only one of those words can stand alone as the answer to our question: μαθηταί — "disciples know." Now we may look for a complement by asking, "Disciples know who(m) or what?" The question is sensible, and the answer is ταῦτα ("these things"). The kernel, then, put into Subject-Verb-Complement order, is μαθηταὶ ἔγνωσαν ταῦτα — "disciples know these things."

In sentence diagramming, a clause's kernel elements are mapped out on what we will call a *baseline*, a horizontal line punctuated with vertical dividers, as illustrated below.

```
 [subject]  |  [verb]  |  [complement]
_____
            |
```

The subject/predicate divider extends below the baseline to symbolize the fact that it represents the major division within the clause. Within the predicate, the verb/comple-ment divider comes down to, but not below the baseline, indicat-

---

[7] Sometimes it can be difficult to identify the main clause(s). A main clause, or independent clause, is one that is not subordinate to any others within the sentence. As a general pattern, verbs are shown as subordinate in one of two ways: they are written as participles or infinitives, or they are introduced by subordinating words such as subordinating conjunctions or relative pronouns. To find the main clause, locate all the verbs in the sentence (remember that in Greek the verb may be omitted at times, especially when it is a linking verb), and eliminate those which are subordinated in one of these ways. If you work accurately, any remaining verbs will be independent. If there is more than one independent verb, all of them will be coordinate with one another in a compound relationship.

ing a secondary division. So the kernel of our sentence would be diagrammed like this:

| οἱ μαθηταί | ἔγνωσαν | ταῦτα | | the disciples | knew | these things |

The topic of the clause, the subject, is the disciples; what is said about them, the predicate, is that they knew (actually, did not know) these things. The predicate in turn divides into verb and complement, which in this case is a direct object. Notice also that the definite article is written right along with the noun. A highly rigorous diagramming method would treat the article as a modifier to the noun, but in my opinion this is a detail not worthy of the space required to account for it. Some of the longer sentences in the New Testament are difficult to fit onto a single page of diagramming, so space efficiency is a key consideration to me.

The same verse also provides an example of a clause whose verb does not require a complement: ὅτε ἐδοξάσθη Ἰησοῦς — "when Jesus was glorified." The subject and verb are "Jesus was glorified" (notice that we are again retaining the voice, which this time is passive). But the question "Jesus was glorified who(m) or what?" is nonsense. There are any number of sensible questions that might be asked, such as "when?" or "why?" or "how?" or "by whom?" But material answering those questions would be adverbial in nature. The complement answers the question "who(m) or what?" after the verb. Since the question doesn't even make sense, we know that this verb does not take a complement, and our kernel consists in this case of only two elements: subject and verb. So the predicate in this case consists of the verb only; it does not subdivide into verb and complement. The baseline, then, would look like this:

| Ἰησοῦς | ἐδοξάσθη |

Before proceeding with another portion of John 12:16, it will be good to talk about another kind of complement. The complement in our example diagram above is a direct object: it receives the verb's action. But some complements rename or modify the subject rather than being acted upon as an object. This happens most commonly with the linking verbs, and these complements are called *predicate nouns* or *predicate adjectives*.[8] An example is John 12:13, εὐλογημένος ὁ ἐρχόμενος ἐν ὀνόματι κυρίου — "Blessed (is) the one coming in the name of the Lord." In order to symbolize the fact that this kind of

---

[8] Many grammarians prefer to label the complement according to its case, such as *predicate nominative* or *predicate accusative*.

complement renames or modifies the subject, the "vertical" line within the predicate is slanted back toward the subject, so that the diagram looks like this:[9]

```
ὁ ἐρχόμενος  |  (X)  \  εὐλογημένος
─────────────────────────────────────
             |
```

Notice that the elliptical verb is represented by (X). An alternative is to supply the verb, in Greek or in English, using parentheses or brackets. I like to supply elliptical elements explicitly where it is possible to be certain exactly what the word should be. In this case it is not easy to decide whether the verb should be indicative mood, declaring a fact, or optative mood, declaring a wish, and I simply supply the (X) when in doubt.

Some grammarians prefer to include indirect objects as well as direct objects on the baseline. The convention for doing this is to place the indirect object after the direct object, using a divider that slants toward the indirect object, symbolizing the fact that the verb's action moves toward the indirect object. The end of John 12:16 provides an example:

```
(X) | ἐποίησαν | ταῦτα  /  αὐτῷ
─────────────────────────────────
    |
```

The alternative is to diagram the indirect object as a modifier, as will be shown later.

Diagramming Modifiers

Most of the non-kernel words in a clause are modifiers, modifying either kernel elements or other modifiers. The basic format for diagramming a modifier is to put it beneath the word it modifies (the head word), linked to the head word's slot with a vertical or angled connector. Most diagramming methods specify that various kinds of modifiers should be shown with connecting links having a particular angle. One popular scheme specifies that modifiers containing no verb are indicated with a connector that angles downward to the left, those with a participle or infinitive have a vertical connector, and those with a finite verb have a connector that angles downward to the right. In my opinion, there is some value to this approach; the reader of the diagram gains information about the kind of modifier without having to read and think about the actual words. But I am not certain that the value is enough to offset the space inefficiencies that often result from these constraints. I would not at all discour-

---

[9] Some diagramming methods would insist on displaying the participles differently in order to indicate that they are participles and not nouns. In my opinion such a distinction is not necessary.

age an approach that tosses this scheme to the wind and draws connectors in whatever shape and at whatever angle will give access to blank space on the page. In this article, though, I will adhere to the conventions just outlined. John 12:16 contains two kinds of modifiers: a clausal modifier with a finite verb, introduced by a subordinating conjunction (ὅτε ἐδοξάσθη Ἰησοῦς), and several simple modifiers, of which the main clause has two: αὐτοῦ modifies μαθηταί and τὸ πρῶτον modifies the verb. These modifiers are diagrammed as follows:

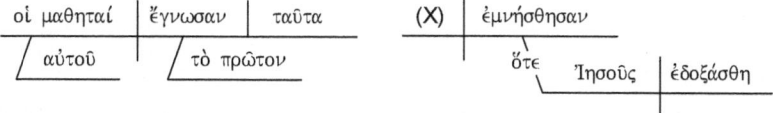

Notice that the subordinating conjunction introducing the clausal modifier is written on the angled connector link. This is standard practice for writing conjunctions: write them on top of the connecting link.

Modifiers that use verbs may of course have additional kernel elements such as subjects, objects, or predicate nouns or adjectives. In such cases, as in the second example just above, the horizontal line of the modifier is simply treated as a baseline and divided appropriately. Genitive absolute participles (which have their own "subject" apart from the governing clause) and infinitives (which may have a "subject" separate from the governing clause) deserve special mention in this regard. In the case of the absolute participle construction, some grammarians suggest using a dotted line for the vertical connector, as shown in the more complicated diagram below. The text is John 12:37: τοσαῦτα δὲ αὐτοῦ σημεῖα πεποιηκότος ἔμπροσθεν αὐτῶν οὐκ ἐπίστευον εἰς αὐτόν (translated rather literally, "but, he having done so many signs before them, they were not believing in him").

As mentioned above, some grammarians prefer to diagram indirect objects as adverbial modifiers rather than as kernel elements. Some use a special symbol for this function, in which the horizontal line protrudes slightly to the left of the angled connector, as indicated below, using the original example from John 12.

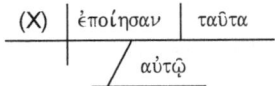

Special Case: Prepositional Phrases. Because prepositions take objects, an additional element is used in this kind of modifier: a vertical divider separating the preposition from the object. John 12:16 has one prepositional phrase, which is diagrammed as follows:

ταῦτα | ἦν γεγραμμένα
/ ἐπ' | αὐτῷ

In some contexts it is clear that the prepositional phrase modifies the verb, in others (such as where the phrase intervenes between article and noun) it clearly modifies the noun, and in many contexts what it modifies is unclear. I recommend the adverbial connection (modifying the verb) as the default, making other connections only as clearly required.

Special Case: Appositives. An appositive is a kind of modifier supplying an alternative designation for something. Probably the most frequent NT expression using an appositive is "the Lord Jesus Christ." The diagramming convention for an appositive is to put it next to the word it renames, and make the connection with an equals sign as shown.

ὁ κύριος = Ἰησοῦς = Χριστός   or   ὁ κύριος = Ἰησοῦς Χριστός

Since "Jesus Christ" occurs so frequently, I do not generally take the space to indicate the appositional relationship between these two words, as shown in the second example above. If there is a "verbal equals sign" such as the phrase "that is" (τουτ' ἔστιν), diagram those words in place of the equals sign.

Diagramming Introductory Words

Sentences often begin with various kinds of words that serve an introductory function. The most common kinds of introductory words are conjunctions indicating a logical connection to the preceding sentence (such as γάρ and οὖν), interjections (such as ἰδοῦ and ἀμήν), and vocative-case words signifying direct address. I would include in this group the negatives οὐ and μή when, in introducing a question, they indicate the expectation of a positive or negative answer. The basic idea behind the diagramming of these words is to place them above the main clause's baseline, at the left end of the baseline, with a dotted vertical line connecting them to the end point of the baseline. John 12:15 provides an example of an interjection (two alternatives diagrammed), and 12:17 provides an example of an introductory conjunction.

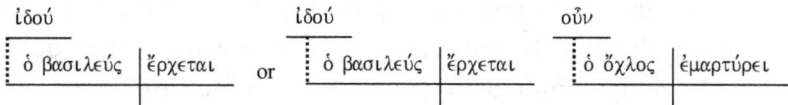

Sometimes a sentence will begin with more than one introductory word, in which case the words may be "stacked" as shown (the example is from John 7:26).

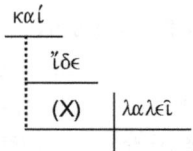

Diagramming Additional Kernel Elements

In addition to the basic kernel elements already covered are a few items encountered only occasionally. Remember that some verbs take a double accusative construction (one a person and one a thing) as their complement, such as John 14:26: ἐκεῖνος ὑμᾶς διδάξει πάντα ("that one will teach you all things"). I like to diagram this construction with a double vertical between the verb and the complement (to show that two accusatives are coming), and then a single vertical between the two accusatives, as in the first example below. Some, however, prefer to use the double vertical with the second, apparently to show that it is the second accusative.

ἐκεῖνος | διδάξει ‖ ὑμᾶς | πάντα   or   ἐκεῖνος | διδάξει | ὑμᾶς ‖ πάντα

Another kind of construction using two accusatives is that in which the second accusative renames the first. It is diagrammed like the double accusative, except that the divider between the two accusatives slants back toward the first so show the predicate relationship of the second to the first. An example of this construction is John 15:15: οὐκέτι λέγω ὑμᾶς δούλους ("no longer do I call you slaves").

(X) | λέγω ‖ ὑμᾶς \ δούλους   or   (X) | λέγω | ὑμᾶς \ δούλους
         \ οὐκέτι   \ οὐκέτι

The difference between these two constructions lies in whether the second accusative is an additional object of the verb (the person-thing variety of double accusative) or whether it renames the one object (the object-predicate variety). One reason I like to use the double vertical after the verb for the person-thing variety is that I can then consistently do the same thing with the object-predicate variety. In the object-predicate construction without the double vertical (see the second example immediately above), the predicate at the end of the baseline almost appears to be renaming the subject. The double vertical before the object helps me recognize the predicate element as an object complement rather than subject complement.

One other special construction involving kernel elements is the periphrastic participle. In this usage, the participle combines with a linking verb to form a phrasal verb unit. Since the participle and the linking verb combine to express the verb of the clause, it makes best sense to write both words in the verb slot of the baseline. The two best approaches regarding the order in which to write the words seem to me to be either always to put the linking verb first or to retain the order in which the words appear in the text. Our example from John 12:16 contains a periphrastic pluperfect, ἦν γεγραμμένα, which has already been shown in previous diagrams.

Subordinate Clause Constructions
Requiring Special Treatment

An example of an adverbial subordinate clause has already been given ("when Jesus was glorified"). Some subordinate clauses, though, are not adverbial, and they require different treatment. These include noun clauses, relative clauses (sometimes called adjective clauses), and quotations. Also, the conjunction ὡς frequently introduces highly elliptical clauses that can be challenging to fill out.

Noun Clauses

A noun clause is a subordinate clause that functions as a noun within its governing clause. Noun clauses most often provide the subject or the object of their governing verbs. Most commonly they are introduced by ὅτι,[10] occasionally by ἵνα[11] or another conjunction, and sometimes with no conjunction at all. Our example from John 12:16 contains a noun clause, ὅτι ταῦτα ἦν ἐπ᾽ αὐτῷ

---

[10] In this usage, ὅτι has the sense "that," not "because."

[11] In this usage, ἵνα does not express purpose and is therefore translated "that" rather than "in order that."

γεγραμμένα, which expresses the object of "they remembered." The problem that noun clauses present is that they *contain* kernel elements and yet at the same time they function *as* a kernel element of another clause. They are "kernels within kernels," and we must find a way to show clearly which words belong to which kernel. One of the fundamental considerations of sentence diagramming is that each kernel requires its own baseline. It follows, then, that a noun clause needs a separate baseline from that of its governing clause. The common diagramming convention for providing a separate baseline is to write the noun clause's baseline above that of the governing clause, and connect the two with a special upright connector that we may call a stilt. The lower end of the stilt rests in whichever slot of the main clause the noun clause supplies (object clauses are more common than subject clauses). Since the main word of any clause is the verb, I like to bring the stilt up under the verb of the noun clause. As usual, the conjunction is written on top of the connector, as shown below. The special stilt symbol makes it easy to avoid trying to read the diagram as though the lower clause were modifying the upper one. It gives the appearance that the upper clause grows out of the lower one and is therefore subordinate to it, as is in fact the case.

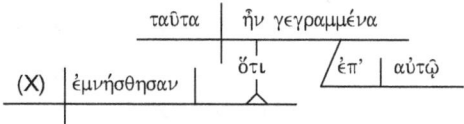

Indirect discourse participles and infinitives are a common form of noun clause and should be diagrammed in this way, although they are not introduced by a conjunction. The same is true of subject infinitives with verbs such as δεῖ and ἔξεστιν.

Quotations

Quotations (assuming that they are long enough to constitute at least a clause) are a variety of noun clause and may be diagrammed as such. For example, in the sentence, "Jesus said, 'I am the good shepherd,'" the quotation functions as the object of "said." Remember the "who(m) or what?" question? Jesus said whom or what? The quotation answers that question. It is also possible for a quotation to be the subject. This is especially common with the expression, "It is written," as in "It is written, 'Man shall not live by bread alone,'" The verb is "is written" (passive voice). Who or what is written? The quotation express the subject, specifying what is written.

Of course, some quotations are very long. Try diagramming the whole Sermon on the Mount as the direct object of λέγων in Matthew 5:2! Because of the length of some quotations, it is useful to follow a practice in which a quotation's stilt moves downward rather than upward from its slot in the governing clause. Then the diagram can simply continue until the and of its sentence, and the next sentence will begin a new diagram in sequence. If a quotation consists of more than one sentence, the diagram will not be able to show that the remaining sentences belong to the quotation, but that is not really a problem. We have already accepted the fact that sentence diagrams cannot show thought flow across a sequence of sentences, and longer quotations simply come under this recognized limitation. John 12:19 provides a good example: οἱ οὖν Φαρισαῖοι εἶπαν πρὸς ἑαυτούς· θεωρεῖτε ὅτι οὐκ ὠφελεῖτε οὐδέν ("Therefore the Pharisees said to themselves, 'You see that you are not benefiting at all.'")

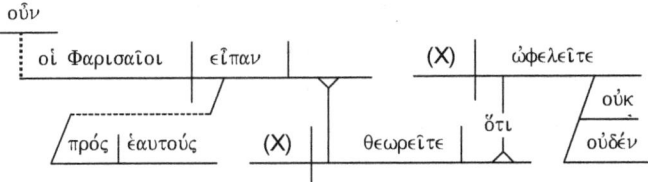

Notice the placement of the prepositional phrase: the dotted horizontal line represents an extender enabling a piece of the diagram to be shifted to another part of the page. Dotted-line extenders should be placed *in the middle* of the link they are extending. In other words, the link should begin and end as usual, and the extender should comprise the center portion. There is no reason an extender could not have a fairly complex shape, if necessary, to reach a blank spot on the page. It is common practice, however, to use line segments rather than curves for this purpose.

Relative (Adjective) Clauses

Relative clauses are sometimes called adjective clauses because, just as noun clauses function as nouns, these function as adjectives. The problems we face with relative clauses are what to do with the relative pronoun and how to connect the clause to the word it modifies adjectivally.

Students commonly stumble over the function of relative pronouns, erroneously identifying them as modifying their antecedents. So, regarding the sentence, "The Savior who loves us reigns," many students would want to say that "who" modifies "Savior." The way the construction works, though, is that the whole clause "who loves us" is the modifier of "Savior"; within that relative clause, "who" is the subject of "loves." That this way of viewing the construction is correct becomes apparent if we consider a similar sentence in which the relative pronoun is the object of its clause rather than the subject: "The Savior whom we love reigns." If the first example were written out in Greek, both *Savior* and *who* would be in the nominative case, seeming to warrant the student's conclusion that *who* modifies *Savior*. But if the second sentence were put into Greek, *Savior* will be nominative, but *whom* will be accusative. We no longer have the grammatical agreement we would need in order for the pronoun to function attributively to *Savior*. The accusative case of the pronoun, however, is perfectly consistent with basic pronoun grammar: a pronoun agrees with its antecedent (the word it refers to, or takes the place of) in gender and number, but its case will ordinarily reflect its usage within its own clause rather than agreeing with the antecedent. So *whom* will be accusative case because it is the direct object of *love*. When we diagram the relative clause, then, we must diagram *whom* as the object of *love*.

And yet we must somehow show that this clause modifies *Savior*. The normal convention for relative clauses is to diagram the clause completely disconnected from the remainder of the sentence, and then connect the relative pronoun's slot to the antecedent's slot with a dotted line or curve. It is best if the connector can be a simple shape and avoid passing directly over other sentence elements. John 12:9 provides a simple example: ...ἵνα τὸν Λάζαρον ἴδωσιν ὃν ἤγειρεν ἐκ νεκρῶν ("that they may see Lazarus, whom he raised from the dead").

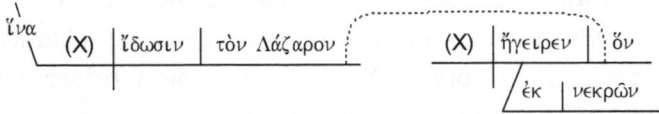

Sometimes the relative pronoun's antecedent is elliptical and must be supplied. A good example of this appears in John 11:46: καὶ εἶπαν αὐτοῖς ἃ ἐποίησεν Ἰησοῦς ("and they told them [the things] which Jesus did"). The antecedent should be shown with the (X) that regularly stands for elliptical elements (or else, following many grammarians, supply an appropriate form of ἐκεῖνος), and the relative clause should then be diagrammed as usual, as shown below. One of the most important things to remember is that the relative pronoun regularly if not always belongs to the clause it introduces, not the one it follows.

Ὡς Clauses

Clauses introduced by ὡς are often highly elliptical and are sometimes challenging to fill out. Often the ὡς clause has only a single word actually expressed, as in John 15:6: ...ἐβλήθη ἔξω ὡς τὸ κλῆμα ("...he is cast out as the branch"). One of two approaches will almost always produce an acceptable result. Probably most grammarians prefer whenever possible to repeat within the ὡς clause the preceding verb and any essential modifiers: "He is cast out as the branch [is cast out]." Notice the elliptical elements supplied (indicated as elliptical by parentheses; square brackets would serve equally well) in the following diagram:

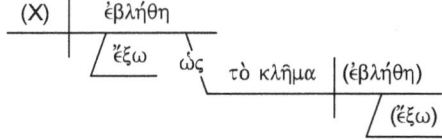

Sometimes, however, this approach will not work grammatically. In John 1:32, John the Baptist testifies, τεθέαμαι τὸ πνεῦμα καταβαῖνον ὡς περιστεράν ("I beheld the Spirit descending as a dove"). It may seem at first that we could follow the pattern stated above: "I beheld the Spirit descending as a dove [descends]." The grammar, though, simply won't allow it, because "dove" is accusative case. For our elliptical clause to work, "dove" would have to be nominative case, since we have it expressing the subject of the elliptical verb. The accusative case shows that John did not think of "dove" as the subject of its clause. The second approach, which works nicely here, is to supply an elliptical participle from εἰμί with "dove" as its predicate. The participle's referent is πνεῦμα, accusative-case object of τεθέαμαι. So the participle would also be accusative (neuter singular), and the predicate would agree with the word it renames (πνεῦμα) and therefore also be accusative. The sense of the sentence would be "I beheld the Spirit descending as [being] a dove," or "as [though he were] a dove."

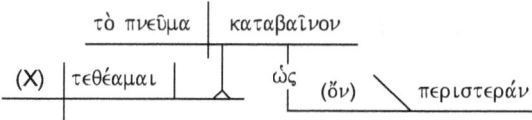

One additional matter to note in this diagram is the indirect discourse participle, diagrammed (as mentioned above) on a stilt in the object slot after the main verb.

Diagramming Special Constructions with the Article

Several constructions with the definite article call for special attention. These include articular infinitives (especially those used as objects of prepositions), articular prepositional phrases, and some pronominal uses of the article. At the root of these constructions lies a question that must be settled about the article's basic function. In the oldest known Greek, ὁ, ἡ, τό is actually a demonstrative pronoun and not an article at all. As such, it carried the full range of noun functions. Over time, the word began to take on new usages, and it eventually it comes, rather than functioning as a noun, to qualify nouns and other expressions in a way that signals a focus on individual identity. In NT Greek the article, with infrequent but not rare exceptions, qualifies other words rather than functioning as a noun that is qualified in turn *by* other words. Whenever possible, then, in my opinion, it is best to attach the article to the word it governs rather than diagram it in its own slot with a modifier attached. Clarifying examples will appear below.

Articular Infinitives

Infinitives are verb forms and therefore appear in verb slots on baselines. The infinitive often has the definite article, however, and the article looks rather strange in the verb slot of a baseline.[12] Since infinitives are verbal nouns, we are not far off the mark when we consider an infinitive to be the verb of a noun clause and build it on a stilt. An article can then appear in the noun slot where the infinitive stilt connects. John is not fond of the articular infinitive, except for a few uses in prepositional phrases (to which we will come in a moment), so I must go elsewhere for an example. Paul says in Romans 14:21, καλὸν τὸ μὴ φαγεῖν κρέα ("It is good not to eat meats").

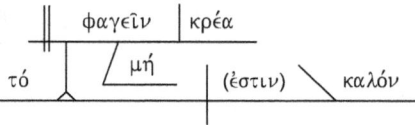

Notice, by the way, that there is a fairly standard convention to identify infinitives by a double vertical that extends below the baseline. To my way of thinking this detail is entirely negotiable.

---

[12] Participles of course can also be articular, but at least an articular participle never has a separate referent occupying a subject slot to the left of the participle. So the article does not look so strange with a participle, and no special conventions are needed for articular participles.

The articular infinitive is especially common in prepositional phrases. John does use a few of these. A good example is 1:48: πρὸ τοῦ σε Φίλιππον φωνῆσαι...εἶδόν σε ("Before Philip called you...I saw you"). Diagramming these constructions as shown below preserves all relevant grammatical features: the preposition is diagrammed with its object phrase, including the article (which in turn connects to the infinitive), and there is room for any possible elements expanding the infinitive clause: accusative of general reference, direct object, vari-various modifiers, etc.

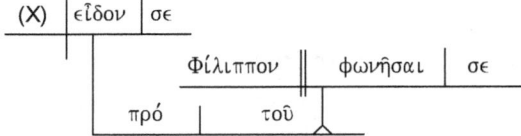

A few infinitive phrases (or clauses) with the genitive article will prove challenging. Most of these may be diagrammed as adverbial, and if the infinitive does not have a subject, simply including the article in the infinitive slot will not look too bad, as in Matthew 3:13: παραγίνεται ὁ Ἰησοῦς...τοῦ βαπτισθῆναι ("Jesus arrives...to be baptized").

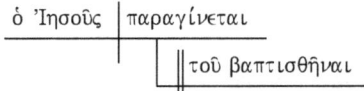

Luke 1:57 (τῇ δὲ Ἐλισάβετ ἐπλήσθη ὁ χρόνος τοῦ τεκεῖν αὐτήν ["And for Elisabeth the time for her to give birth was fulfilled"]) is a more difficult example because the presence of an accusative of general reference makes the infinitive baseline look like a regular baseline, in which an article in the verb slot looks very odd. I understand the infinitive to modify the noun "time" ("the time of her giving birth," rendering the infinitive with an English gerund), and I would diagram as follows:

An example of the fact that every language refuses at some point to submit itself to simple and consistent grammatical rules appears in Acts 10:25: ὡς δὲ ἐγένετο τοῦ εἰσελθεῖν τὸν Πέτρον... ("And when it came about that Peter entered..."). The infinitive phrase must provide the subject, otherwise the verb is left without a subject. Furthermore, it happens often that γίνομαι in this sense has an infinitive as its subject. But the genitive article is a monkey wrench in the grammatical works; the article with a subject infinitive, according to strict grammatical principle, should be nominative (as in the example above from Romans 14:21). I do not find an objection-free way to diagram this verse; until I come across something better I will hold my nose and write the genitive article in the subject slot, as follows:

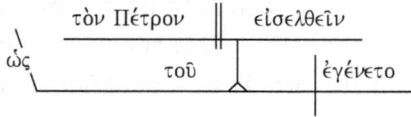

Articular Prepositional Phrases

Prepositional phrases can also be articular, but the question arises where to place the article. Placing it in the preposition slot makes it appear that it qualifies only the preposition. When the articular phrase is substantival, the article could conceivably be diagrammed as carrying the noun function alone and the phrase could be diagrammed as its modifier. But this seems to me to be a poor reflection of the fact that the article actually qualifies the whole phrase, as explained earlier. Furthermore, sometimes the articular phrase is attributive; in such a case the whole phrase, including the article, must somehow appear as a modifier to the head word. The best way I know to handle all the various constructions consistently is to treat the prepositional phrase somewhat like a noun clause by building it on a stilt. A substantival example comes from John 5:28: πάντες οἱ ἐν τοῖς μνημείοις ἀκούσουσιν τῆς φωνῆς αὐτοῦ ("All the ones in the tombs will hear his voice"). An attributive example comes from John 12:21: οὗτοι...προσῆλθον Φιλίππῳ τῷ ἀπὸ Βηθσαϊδά ("These came to Philip who was from Bethsaida").

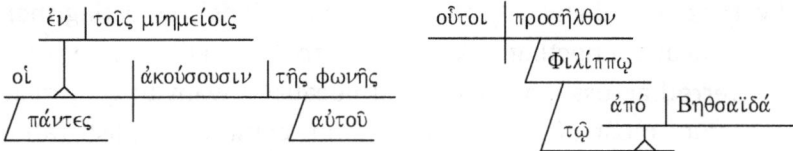

Substantival Genitive Phrases Governed by an Article

Every student who passes first-year Greek learns that a Greek adjective can function as a noun (the substantive use) and that this construction is usually articular. Also elementary is the fact that the genitive case most often functions in an adjectival way. It is not surprising, then, that we can find instances of a substantival construction with the genitive case instead of an adjective. This construction often consists of article + article^{genitive} + noun^{genitive}, where the first article is in the case appropriate to the function of the phrase.

I see two options for diagramming this construction. One approach would be to treat it like a substantival adjective: simply write the whole phrase, article(s) and all, in a single diagram slot. The second approach is to let the article stand alone and diagram the genitive phrase as its modifier. This approach runs contrary to the preference stated earlier to treat the article as a qualifier of its phrase rather than as a head word modified by something else. But that preference cannot be maintained as an absolute, because there are places where the article's function is so compellingly pronominal that there simply is no other option than to diagram it in a noun slot alone. The most frequent such construction is where, in narrative, the bare nominative article, followed by δέ, serves to switch the narrative focus back to a previously known party who is the subject of the new sentence. Since the predisposition against the pronominal article cannot be maintained absolutely, I see no problem with treating the article as a pronoun in other constructions where no preferable alternative presents itself. Romans 14:19 provides a good example: τὰ τῆς εἰρήνης διώκωμεν ("Let us pursue the things of peace.")

$$(X) \mid \text{διώκωμεν} \mid \text{τὰ τῆς εἰρήνης} \quad \text{or} \quad (X) \mid \text{διώκωμεν} \mid \text{τά} \,/\, \text{τῆς εἰρήνης}$$

Diagramming Coordinate Relationships

As one would expect, the conventions for diagramming coordinate relationships display the coordinate elements in a visually parallel arrangement. The items are stacked vertically, and any coordinating conjunctions connecting them are written on the vertical connecting link. Because the concepts are straightforward, easily transferred across languages, and because I want to give many examples, I will construct most of my examples from common English rather than Biblical texts. Take the statement, "I ate chicken and rice." The object part of the sentence (which answers "I ate whom or what?") is a series of two coordinate items rather than a single item. In "I ate quickly and drank slowly," the coordinate items are the verbs. In "She and I ate gratefully," the coordinate items are the subjects.

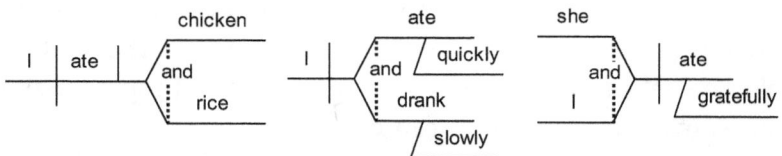

Coordinate series may often be broken down into subsets. Take, for example, "I ate chicken and rice and cake and ice cream." Grammatically there is a single series of four, but some clarity of detail can be gained by breaking the series apart into two pairs, since the first two are obviously the main course and the second two are obviously the dessert. The diagram would look like this:

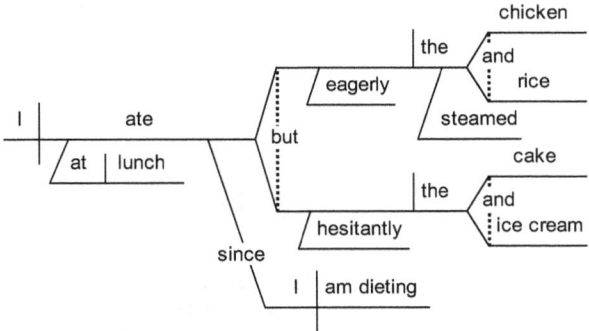

When a modifier describes all the elements in a coordinate series, it is best to diagram the modifier linked to a point on the diagram just to the left of where the coordination bracket splits. Take this more complex sentence: "At lunch I ate the steamed chicken and rice eagerly, but the cake and ice cream hesitantly, since I am dieting." *At lunch* modifies the entire predicate with all four objects. *Steamed* modifies *chicken and rice* but not the verb, and certainly not *cake and ice cream! Eagerly* modifies *ate the chicken and rice* but not *ate the cake and ice cream*; vice-versa with *hesitantly*. *Since I am dieting* clearly modifies *ate the cake and ice cream hesitantly*, but on careful thought it also seems to make good sense as an explanation of *ate the chicken and rice eagerly*. I incline toward taking modifiers with all the words that they can reasonably modify, so I will diagram accordingly.

Notice some details. The verb slot of the baseline splits *before* the direct object divider. This allows me separate places on the verb slot from which to drop adverbial modifiers (*eagerly* and *hesitantly*) so that they modify the verb as construed with only one set of objects. The left-hand portion of the verb slot, prior to splitting, gives me a place where I can drop modifiers for the verb as construed with all the objects. The articles are located just to the left of the division of each object slot, so that the articles qualify both words in their respective object pairs. The modifier *steamed* connects to the left of the division point so that it modifies both *chicken* and *rice*. If the sentence had said "baked chicken and fried rice," the diagramming provides a place for the two adjectives to be dropped below their respective nouns.

A special kind of coordination exists where there is a more intense pairing signaled by *pairs* of conjunctions or other words uniting the two elements. The most common such pairs are "both...and," "on the one hand (μέν)...on the other (δέ)," "either...or," "not (only)...but (also)," and "neither...nor."[13] These pairs are diagrammed with the two conjunctions stacked together in the regular conjunction slot. The idea is that the top conjunction goes with the top word and the bottom with the bottom. So "I ate not only my steak but her chicken" would be diagrammed:

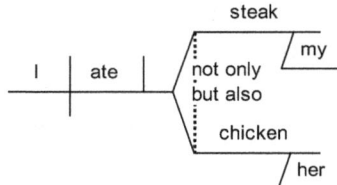

Since our example passage John 12:16 contains an instance of simple coordination and also an instance of this more intense coordination, and since we are nearing the end of the article, I will now give a complete diagram of the whole sentence.

---

[13] I think it is good *not* to consider as coordinate pairs the conditional construction "if...then" and the comparative construction "just as...so also." In both of these constructions, the first clause is actually subordinate to the second and should be diagrammed accordingly. "If" and "just as" would be diagrammed as subordinating conjunctions. "Then" ordinarily does not even occur as a separate word in Greek; "so also" can be diagrammed adverbially.

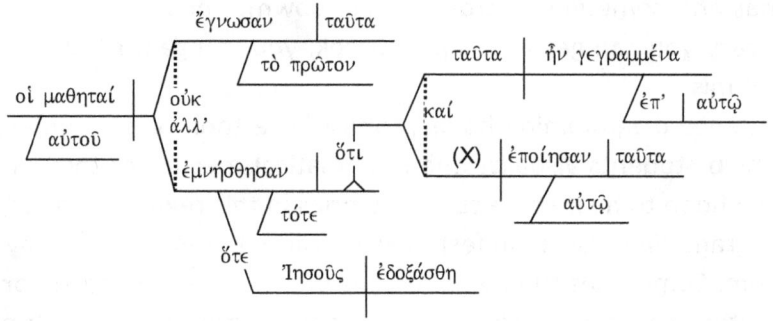

One special situation involving coordination requires attention. The word καί contracts with certain other words in a phenomenon called *crasis*. It is perfectly legitimate, indeed necessary, to break these contractions into their sepa-separate words for diagramming purposes. John 12:32 is a good example: κἀγὼ ἐὰν ὑψωθῶ ἐκ τῆς γῆς, πάντας ἑλκύσω πρὸς ἐμαυτόν ("And I, if I should be lifted up from the earth, will draw all to myself"). Notice how κἀγώ has been broken down into its components, καί and ἐγώ, in order to diagram the conjunction and the pronoun in their respective places.

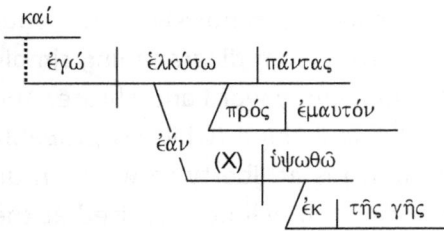

Conclusion

Diagramming is obviously not easy, but for those with a reasonable mastery of Greek grammar, it is certainly doable. Of course, this article by no means covers every sort of situation that you will encounter, but it does give a reasonably complete picture of the kinds of things you will have to do. Improvisation will often be necessary, and you should not hesitate to do something you can't quite find in any textbooks if you are convinced that it is the clearest way to show the grammar as you understand it. Obviously there is no body of diagramming legislation that you can go to prison for violating, nor must your diagrams be worthy of immortalizing in stone in order to be of any value at all, and you should realize of course that there is always room for growth in understanding and consequent revision. So why not give sentence diagramming a try? You can even do it in English if your Greek is not strong (though English grammar seems to me "fuzzier" than Greek grammar and sometimes harder to nail down). Though you won't gain quite the accuracy you can get working in Greek, you can gain much that you would otherwise miss.

I believe sentence diagramming holds promise as a tool for elementary Greek teachers to help students visualize the grammatical mechanics they are attempting to learn. I hope to hear some success stories in this regard in coming years. Sentence diagramming also manifests exegetical value in various ways beyond the classroom. Sometimes the combinations of coordination and subordination of ideas within sentences will suggest possible bases for expository sermon outlines. Sometimes new understanding of a passage will dawn as you try to discern exactly how these words relate to one another, and the resulting diagram will actually record a valuable discovery. The better you get at Greek grammar, though, the less often the diagram will represent new discovery, because the details you previously had to labor to understand now come to you at first reading. You may come to view diagramming as unnecessary, but when you stop to think about it, you will realize that *doing* the diagramming is what eventually made it unnecessary. If you had never labored through passages in this way, you would not now be reading them so accurately so quickly. But, if your experience is like mine, you will still enjoy and profit from diagramming simply because it forces you to slow down and think about every word and phrase. And when the diagramming itself comes fairly easily, your mind (which is probably capable of more multi-tasking than you are aware) is at liberty to work on dimensions of the passage beyond the grammatical. You will be surprised at the wonderful truths you will find in Scripture that cannot be put into a sentence diagram but that you may never have found if the diagramming process had not slowed you down enough to notice them.

Diagramming Policies for the BibleWorks Greek New Testament Sentence Diagrams

by

Randy A. Leedy

Introduction

This document is intended as a fairly comprehensive description of the diagramming policies I followed in preparing the BibleWorks Greek New Testament Sentence Diagrams. It is not a primer on diagramming method; a separate document fills that need, with which this document assumes that the reader is already familiar. Neither is it a grammar textbook; it assumes that the reader already has a solid working knowledge of Greek grammar. While I recognize that not all the users of the diagrams will by any means be expert grammarians, it is not possible for me to assume responsibility for teaching grammar within the scope of this project. Hopefully those whose development is lacking but whose instincts are true will be able to progress by drawing valid inferences from the diagrams and the supporting materials.

The purpose of this document is to state policies governing the choices made in cases where the grammar is complex and in matters where more than one approach is possible. The organization scheme reflects the kinds of questions with which I anticipate that a user will consult this document. Some will be seeking information about a particular diagramming symbol, others a particular grammatical construction, others a particular Greek word, etc. This scheme will provide abundant opportunity for overlapping discussions. While often referring the reader to other parts of the document for additional information, especially where the discussion elsewhere is lengthy, I have allowed a good bit of that overlap to stand for the sake of the reader's convenience.

Sections of this document are numbered with Roman numerals for the main divisions and Arabic numerals for the subdivisions in order to facilitate reference from one portion of the document to another.

I. Policies governing the general layout of the diagrams

I.1) The textual base for the diagrams the 28th edition of the Nestle-Aland text (hereafter referred to as NA28).

I.2) The diagrams are of the Reed-Kellogg type, essentially following the method and symbology outlined by John D. Grassmick in *Principles and Practice of Greek Exegesis*, published by Dallas Theological Seminary.

I.3) Each diagram contains a single sentence, generally following the punctuation of NA28. Occasionally I follow a strong consensus of versions rather than NA28. Also, there are times when the punctuation of NA28 divides the text so that a new sentence lacks a governing clause. This especially happens in longer passages featuring relative clauses, such as in Ephesians 1. I do not hesitate to ignore sentence punctuation in NA28 where it appears to me that what they mark as a new sentence is grammatically subordinate to the previous material and belongs in a single longer sentence for diagramming purposes.

I.4) Since many sentences extend over several verses and some verses contain more than one sentence, verse divisions are not carefully delineated. I have indicated in the left margin of the diagrams what verses each diagram covers. There is no attempt within the longer diagrams to indicate verse divisions, and portions of a verse are sometimes separated rather widely from one another on the page because of the complexity of the grammar.

I.5) No provision is made within the diagrams for tracing the order of words in the text. The diagrams are meant to be read alongside the text (whether on paper or in the mind), not in place of the text.

I.6) Wherever possible, diagrams are drawn to fit on a single page, to facilitate printing. In those few cases where a page break is unavoidable, the break falls at some substantial syntactical break point.

I.7) Because many NT sentences are quite long, compactness is given great priority, again in the interest of suitability for printing and, even more importantly, of maximizing the amount of a sentence that is visible on the computer monitor without scrolling. It is obviously impossible to format the diagrams to every user's preference, and I decided that compactness would be the most widely valued virtue. However, I did not wish to push compactness to the point of compromising clarity, so the font size is adequate, and the diagrams always leave enough white space to allow sections of the sentences to stand out with adequate distinctness.

II. Policies governing capitalization, punctuation, accents, and variant spellings

II.1) Capitalization of proper names is retained, but no other capitalization is used. Words capitalized in order to signal the beginning of a section or of a direct quotation are often buried in the middle of the diagram, so to retain the capitalization would serve no useful purpose, and the capital letters would look distracting within the diagrams.

II.2) Since the words in the sentence diagram reflect the order of words in the text so imperfectly, punctuation, like capitalization, seems pointless. So all commas, colons, periods, question marks, and parentheses are omitted from the diagrams. (Words enclosed in parentheses within the diagrams are elliptical words supplied according to policies discussed later in this document.) Sometimes I depart from NA28 punctuation, as discussed in section I.3.

II.3) Square brackets within the NA28 text, which are text-critical indicators and not punctuation marks, are retained. This results in some visual awkwardness, because where more than one word is enclosed in brackets, the word with the left bracket and the word with the right bracket may well be separated from one another in the diagram.

II.4) Accents present some rather tricky considerations. The grave accent is used only in running text; the rule is that an acute accent on the last syllable of a word that is followed by another word, with no intervening punctuation, changes to grave unless some special consideration applies. Therefore, to allow the grave accent to remain on individual words in their diagramming slots is inappropriate. Of course where a word slot within a diagram contains a multi-word phrase, the grave accent on any except the last word of the phrase would be appropriate. Thus, τὸν θεόν is fine, but τὸν θεὸν or τόν θεόν are not. Grave accents in the NA28 text are replaced with the acute within the diagrams on words that are the only or the last word in their slot. The other major factor related to accents is deciding how to deal with enclitics and proclitics, which ordinarily lose their accent in running text. It would not be wise to restore the normal accent for these words, because, for example, the articles ὁ and ἡ, if accented ὅ and ἥ, would be rendered indistinguishable from relative pronouns. The reasonable options are either to let the accents stand as they are in the text or to omit the accent from enclitics and proclitics. To let the accents stand as they are in the text would cause the same problem as letting the grave accent stand: apart from running text some of those accents would be inappropriate. The policy, therefore, is to omit the accent from enclitics and proclitics. Most commonly, of course, these words appear in the text without their accent, and omitting the accent in these cases is the natural thing to do. But even where the words do retain their accent in the text, the accent is removed in the diagrams for the sake of consistency. The exceptions are the genitive, dative, and accusative of the second person personal pronouns in the singular when the accent appears to be retained to signal emphasis (σοῦ, σοί and σέ), and the special form ἔστιν, which, accented on the penult, is actually not an enclitic at all. Further, the additional accent sometimes picked up by the word preceding an enclitic is also omitted in the diagrams. For further discussion of the principles of accentuation for these words one may consult D. A. Carson's *Greek Accents: A Student's Manual* or another textbook that explains accents. Occasional errors in applying these policies regarding accents have no doubt crept into the diagrams, and help in identifying and eliminating them will be appreciated.

II.5) The spelling of some words varies depending on what sound comes next. Common examples are ἐκ / ἐξ, ἀπό / ἀπ' / ἀφ', and οὐ / οὐκ / οὐχ. Rarely if ever will one of these words be followed in the same diagramming slot by another word that would require a spelling different from that in the text. While there is something to be said for eliminating the variant spellings and always using the base form, I opted to retain the form used in the text to minimize difficulty for the reader who might be confused by not being able to find in the diagram precisely the same word that appears in the text.

III. Policies governing the choice of diagramming symbols

Many of the choices are obvious: adjective, adverb, prepositional phrase, etc. In some cases, however, a word's function does not match its part of speech. For example, Mat. 4:17 reads ἀπὸ τότε ἤρξατο ὁ Ἰησοῦς κηρύσσειν.... The word τότε is an adverb, but here it has a noun-like function, serving as the object of the preposition. One might suggest expanding the number of available symbols in order to have a symbol perfectly suited for every conceivable situation. The drawback to such an approach, however, is that there are often ambiguities in expression so that more than one symbol could be defended as appropriate. The more symbols, the more trouble one has deciding which to use. Is having to find some systematic basis to govern choices from among more than one potentially appropriate symbol a lesser difficulty than sometimes having to use a less-than-ideal symbol? In my judgment it is not, and so, valuing the relative simplicity of the time-honored Reed-Kellogg symbology (or reasonably close approximations of it), I have not expanded the symbol set with new items of my own private devising.

III.1) Awareness of baseline conventions is assumed and is not discussed here. The accompanying "how-to" document mentioned above discusses these conventions in detail.

III.2) *General conventions regarding subordinate elements.* Many symbols for modifiers appear in two forms: one with a vertical upright connector and one with the connector slanting downward to the left. Symbols with vertical connectors are used for modifiers containing a participle or infinitive; the slanted version is for modifiers that do not contain these verbals. Modifiers containing finite verbs use the subordinate clause symbol that slants downward to the right. A noun clause is connected by a vertical stilt (a *standard* in Grassmick's terminology) to the slot for the noun in whose place it functions, usually the object or the subject slot.

III.3) Simple negatives (οὐ[κ,χ] and μή) introducing questions and signaling what answer is expected are diagrammed on an interjection symbol. Negative adverbs (e.g. μηκέτι) can have a dual function of signaling the expected answer and also supplying adverbial material. I diagrammed these words as adverbs, opting to tolerate the loss of the indication of the introductory function rather than complicate the diagrams by dividing the words and diagramming the parts separately.

III.4) The indirect object symbol is used only with transitive verbs. Some datives even with transitive verbs seem to function less as objects than as indicators of personal interest. Personal interest is diagrammed on an adverb symbol rather than as an indirect object. Unfortunately, I do not find it possible to distinguish between these two uses of the dative with clear objectivity. One point of inconsistency arises here: Grassmick specifies the use of vertical uprights for all modifiers containing participles or infinitives, but his only indirect object symbol has a slanted upright. Grassmick does not specify how to diagram a substantive participle functioning as indirect object, and his illustrative diagramming of the book of Colossians does not contain any such participles. I considered using a right-angle indirect object symbol for these participles, but I felt that the presence of the leftward-jutting stub was the crucial detail to retain. While on the topic of the indirect object, I will add that I think it is worthwhile to consider including the indirect object on the baseline, with the upright divider slanting from lower left to upper right, symbolizing motion in the direction of the indirect object. For reasons too detailed to discuss here, I chose not to diagram in that fashion.

III.5) The direct object symbol is used for complementary participles and infinitives, even where the verb is not transitive (e.g. after δύναμαι). A good alternative would be to place the complementary verbal's stilt in the same slot as the verb, with no upright divider between verb and complement.

III.6) The predicate noun/adjective symbol is used on the baseline immediately after the verb for subject complements; the same symbol after an object indicates an object complement. There is a predicate genitive that differs a little from the usual predicate noun/adjective construction in that it has a genitive-case relationship (usually possession) to the subject rather than a simple renaming or attributive connection (e.g., αὐτῶν ἐστιν ἡ βασιλεία τῶν οὐρανῶν in Mat. 5:3). For this predicate genitive I used the simple "predicate noun/adjective" symbol.

III.7) For the second accusative in the double accusative construction consisting of a person and a thing (e.g. Mat. 21:24: ἐρωτήσω ὑμᾶς λόγον ἕνα), I used a symbol that looks like a direct object symbol but has a closely spaced double upright divider.

III.8) Sometimes it is difficult to decide whether to diagram an accusative and an infinitive as the double accusative (described above) or as indirect discourse. The main criteria are two. First, does the verb take the double accusative construction with two nouns? If so, then the construction is diagrammed as such even when the second noun is an infinitive. Second, does the person in the accusative function more as the object of the verb or as the subject of the infinitive? This criterion comes into play with παρακαλέω, where the person seems to me very often to be as much the object of the verb as the subject of the infinitive—if not more so. It does not seem quite right to read the construction as, for example, Paul exhorting "that you do such-and-such," which seems to me to miss a certain focus on Paul's exhorting *you*. (Note: participle indirect discourse is different from infinitive indirect discourse in that the infinitive is a verbal noun while the participle is a verbal adjective; therefore, the infinitive can be used in the double accusative construction where the participle cannot.)

III.9) The noun clause symbol (an upward moving stilt) is used for noun clauses that are not direct or indirect quotations (see below regarding quotations). The bottom of the stilt (the triangular portion) rests in the slot that the noun clause fills, and the top of the stilt connects to the verb slot on the baseline of the noun clause or to the left end of the conjunction symbol for a compound construction.

III.10) Quotations are a special form of noun clause. Most commonly they function as the direct object of verbs such as "He said." They can also function as the subject; especially common is the passive γέγραπται with the quotation as its subject. Short quotations can easily be diagrammed using the standard convention for noun clauses: build the quotation on a stilt resting in the subject or object slot as appropriate. But what about long quotations? Try diagramming the whole Sermon on the Mount as the object of λέγων in Mat. 5:2! The obvious thing to do is diagram the remainder of the sentence containing the verb of speaking or writing as the object of its verb and then simply start a new diagram at the first sentence break. This approach can be enhanced by using an "upside down" stilt for quotations so that the reader's progress through the passage is not hindered by the sentence break. This approach also minimizes the vertical distance between the noun slot to which the quotation connects and the beginning clause of the quotation. One might be justified in using upward stilts for quotations that do not extend beyond the sentence break and downward stilts for those that do. However, occasionally it is not clear where the quotation ends; e.g. in John 3, where does the record of Jesus' words to Nicodemus end and the evangelist's voice resume? And it does seem more consistent always to move the same direction with quotations, rather than sometimes moving one direction and sometimes the other. So the policy I have followed is to use the downward-moving stilt for all quotations of any length, whether direct or indirect (after all, it is sometimes impossible to tell whether ὅτι should be construed as introducing direct or indirect discourse).

III.11) The substantival infinitive symbol (an infinitive symbol resting atop an upward-moving stilt) is used where the infinitive has a noun use and needs a stilt. The most common such uses are subject, direct object (including the complementary use after certain verbs such as δύναμαι) and indirect discourse; also the use as an appositive is not terribly rare.

III.12) The appositive symbol is fairly straightforward in most cases: a simple equals sign between single words (with their articles and modifiers) joined in apposition. When larger units are joined in apposition, each is placed within the "brackets" symbol, and the equals sign joins them.

III.13) Sometimes the text contains wording functioning as a verbal equals sign (especially the phrase τοῦτ ἔστιν). In these cases the verbal expression substitutes for the equals sign to establish the appositional connection.

III.14) I use several symbols for prepositional phrases, depending on details of the construction. The standard prepositional phrase functioning as a modifier, whether adjectival or adverbial, uses the symbol with the slanting upright connecting to the head word and a vertical upright between the preposition and its object. When the object of the preposition is a participle or an infinitive, the symbol used is identical to the standard one except that the connecting upright is vertical.

III.15) Sometimes prepositional phrases are introduced by an article signaling an attributive or a substantive construction. Where to place that article is a challenging question. Grassmick did a variety of things where this construction appears in Colossians: 1:20; 1:23 (where his diagramming appears very weak to me); 2:1; 3:2,5; 4:7,8,12,13,16. Where the articular prepositional phrase does not modify some substantive, the question arises whether the article itself carries a substantive function, modified by the prepositional phrase (which is how Grassmick diagrams) or whether the article marks the prepositional phrase as itself substantive. In my opinion, either approach is defensible for this construction. But where the articular prepositional phrase modifies a noun (as in Col. 3:5—τὰ μέλη τὰ ἐπὶ τῆς γῆς), it seems clear to me that the article should be diagrammed along with the prepositional phrase as a single adjectival modifier. Grassmick is able to make the prepositional phrase modify the article in that passage only by supplying an elliptical μέλη in apposition to the explicit one, which strikes me as a dubious approach. It seems much better to me in both constructions simply to put the article in the noun slot (for the substantive construction) or the adjective slot (for the attributive construction) and then build the prepositional phrase on a stilt resting on that same slot. This approach to the diagramming binds the article and the prepositional phrase into a noun or adjective unit. Examples of the substantival construction in Colossians (to match Grassmick) include 1:20, 2:1, 3:2, and 4:7,8,13,16; the adjectival construction appears in 1:23, 3:5, and 4:12.

III.16) Material completing a preposition is diagrammed as the object of that preposition, regardless of part of speech.

III.17) Substantival participles are diagrammed on stilts. The stilt is necessary where such participles have objects, but many substantival participles lack further baseline material. In those cases I would have preferred to place the participle directly into its noun slot without the stilt, but some considerations regarding consistent use of the diagramming symbols provided in the BibleWorks program environment within which I developed these diagrams led me to use the stilts consistently, whether necessary or not. A good example of an unnecessary stilt is Mat. 5:4, where οἱ πενθοῦντες could simply rest in the subject slot without the stilt.

III.18) For attributive and adverbial participles, the BibleWorks considerations mentioned immediately above did not apply, and I used simple right-angle modifier symbols, with additional baseline elements attached as appropriate. Note that while the adverbial participle's referent is usually the subject of the governing clause, it is not at all uncommon, especially in more complex writing, for the referent to be some other element of the governing clause. (This assertion contradicts the view Martin Culy, expressed relatively recently, which I consider completely unnecessary and unhelpful and therefore hope that it will gain no lasting traction in the community of students of NT Greek.)

III.19) For the genitive absolute participle and the rare occurrences of the absolute in the other cases, I use a modifier symbol with a dotted vertical segment to call attention to the lack of an ordinary case relation to the governing clause.

III.20) Participles in indirect discourse are diagrammed on a stilt leading to a full baseline on which the participle's referent is diagrammed as the subject and the participle is placed in the verb slot. In these constructions both the participle and its referent together serve as the object of a verb of sensation, thought, or communication. (Thus it is broader than the term *discourse*, which signifies communication, suggests.) If one person hears another person speaking (ptcp.), the object of the verb of hearing is not just the person. It is also the speaking. The person and the action combine to express what is heard. Some cases are challenging. For example, Jesus finds the disciples sleeping (εὑρίσκει αὐτοὺς καθεύδοντας—Mat. 26:40). Is the participle indirect discourse ("sleeping" is part of what He found)? Object complement (He found them *to be* sleeping)? Adverbial (He found them while they were sleeping)? The first two appear to me to be the best choices, and I would go with the first while recognizing the validity of the second. (For further discussion, see the entry for εὑρίσκω in section IX.) After all, if the construction had an adjective rather than a participle, I would go with object complement (e.g. Acts 5:10—εὗρον αὐτὴν νεκράν), although theoretically an ellip- elliptical participle or, more likely an infinitive, from εἰμί could be supplied in order to get an indirect discourse construction.

III.21) The coordinating conjunction symbols are fairly straightforward. Some details are discussed in a separate section on coordination that appears below. A coordination symbol lacking the left-hand stub is used in cases where there is nothing to the left of the coordinate series to which the series can connect. For example, "Jesus spoke, and the crowds listened" would use this symbol to join the two independent clauses. If there were an introductory conjunction or an interjection such as "Behold, Jesus spoke, and the crowds listened," then the conjunction symbol with the stub jutting leftward would be used, to give a connection point for the conjunction or interjection.

III.22) I use two symbols to connect relative pronouns to their antecedents: one a line ("hingeable" in the middle) and one a curve. There is no difference in meaning between the two; I use whatever shape allows the most efficient use of space. One principle I do follow fairly rigidly: the relative pronoun should be to the right of or below the antecedent, or both, whenever possible, and such positioning is almost always possible. These positions more readily reflect grammatical subordination than a position above or to the left would suggest.

III.23) A dotted vertical line is used to indicate pendent (hanging) constructions regardless of the case of the hanging element (which is usually nominative). The pendent element is diagrammed as appropriate and is then connected by the dotted vertical line to the word marking its resumption in the grammatically formed sentence. This construction is discussed in section VII.10 below.

III.24) Extenders. Sometimes the page simply lacks horizontal space for an extensive construction, and one needs a way to position part of the diagram elsewhere on the page than it would ordinarily be. Most of these cases involve modifiers, which I diagram by beginning the vertical or angled portion of the symbol beneath the head word and then, at a point that makes appropriate use of available space, taking that line off at an angle (horizontal if at all possible) with a dotted segment moving to the left or right as necessary to reach an available portion of the page, then resuming the solid vertical or angled portion at its original angle at a length that reaches the space which I want the horizontal part of the symbol containing the diagrammed text to occupy. So these dotted line segments serve to displace a modifier (or noun clause in some cases) symbol from its expected location to some other portion of the page where space is available. Occasionally this convention offsets a horizontal line such as a direct object slot or an appositional construction, but I avoid such diagramming whenever possible.

IV. Policies governing the selection of head words under which to diagram modifiers

IV.1) A modifier seeming to modify a whole idea rather than a single word or phrase is construed with the head word of that idea. Thus, for example, a word that seems to modify the whole predicate of a sentence, including verb and complement, is construed with the verb.

IV.2) Prepositional phrases are construed as modifying the verb except in cases where they *clearly* modify something else (usually a noun). For example, a prepositional phrase embedded between article and noun is clearly attributive to the noun. Also there are cases where the prepositional phrase coheres conceptually much better with a noun or adjective than with the verb.

IV.3) Subordinate clauses almost always modify the verb. Sometimes a "where" clause modifies a noun (e.g. Mat. 28:6), although such a construction could also be diagrammed as a relative clause (as I did at Mat. 6:19-20, an inconsistency that perhaps ought to be resolved).

IV.4) Occasionally an anarthrous participle could be construed as either attributive to an anarthrous noun or as adverbial. Anarthrous participles are construed as attributive only where the superiority of that connection is clear. Of course, an anarthrous substantive is fairly common and is not generally confused with other constructions (e.g. Mat. 3:3 βοῶντος).

IV.5) Καί in the sense "also" presents a challenge. Does it attach to the verb or to some other portion of the sentence? If it attaches to a noun, what symbol should be used? Is it really an adjective? Since καί in this sense indicates an additive relationship, I always look for the parallel thought connection in the preceding context. Which element of this sentence is being added to a parallel element of the preceding context? If the same subject is "also" doing the action of a different verb, then it is the verb that is being added, so I diagram καί as an adverbial modifier to the verb. If another subject is doing the same action someone else in the preceding context did, then I diagram καί as modifying the noun.

IV.6) Negatives are often challenging. The negative always (or at least very nearly always) precedes the word it negates, but not always immediately. I generally construe a negative with the verb unless the context presents a compelling reason to do otherwise. Many clauses place the negative near the beginning, and the negative makes sense with either the verb or some other element located closer to the negative. In general, I understand the early placement of the negative as signaling the negation of the clause as a whole rather than the negation of the specific sentence element that follows, and therefore I diagram the negative as modifying the verb. An exception to what I am describing here is when the negative is the very first word of a question, functioning to signal an expected positive (οὐ) or negative (μή) answer. In these cases I diagram the negative as an interjection, as described in section III.3.

V. Policies governing selection of the points at which the diagramming symbols connect

V.1) Any kind of modifier to a coordinate series connects to the stub of the co-ordinating conjunction symbol, not to the symbol to which the conjunction connects.

V.2) Occasionally a single verb with a compound complement (direct object or predicate noun/adjective) has separate modifiers associated with each complement, such as "He put the paper in the drawer and the pencil on the desk." One approach would be to diagram so that there are two coordinate verbs, one of which is elliptical. This approach provides two separate verbs to accept the separate modifiers. The approach I follow is to diagram just one verb and then to attach the coordinating conjunction symbol to the right end of the verb slot. The complement symbols then attach to the end of each shelf of the conjunction, which is expanded far enough to the right to allow space to connect each adverbial modifier to its conjunction shelf to the left of the complement symbol. The same kind of approach can be taken on the left end of the baseline if there are separate modifiers to the verb associated with different subjects. I did not find this latter construction to be at all common.

V.3) A special problem arises where one expression modifies coordinate verbs that have separate subjects, if either verb also has a complement. In such a construction, the verbs share no point in the diagram at which a modifier can be connected. The least of the evils seems to me to connect the modifier to the left stub of the coordinating conjunction joining the coordinate clauses. The weakness of this approach is that it makes the modifier appear to modify the subjects rather than the verbs. I do not recall, though, any places where the subjects of coordinate verbs actually do share a modifier. So that construction should be understood as indicating that the modifier modifies the clauses as wholes, which implies that they primarily modify the key word of each clause, the verb. An alternative approach that would work well with a short modifier would be to simply diagram it with each verb: as an explicit expression modifying the first verb and as an elliptical expression with the remaining verbs. In the case of a long modifier, though, such as an extended purpose clause, this approach is unworkable. One other alternative would be to diagram the modifier beneath the last of the verbs that it modifies, and then connect it with additional lines to the other verb(s) in the series. This approach would likely involve the weakness of drawing lines on top of other words and diagramming symbols, which could render the diagram a little messy. But at least it would connect the modifier directly with the verbs. I opted, though, to avoid the messiness.

V.4) Introductory words such as conjunctions and interjections connect to the left end of the baseline.

V.5) Introductory conjunctions and interjections or vocatives may be stacked vertically, with the conjunction on top and any interjections or vocatives connected on their left end to the conjunction's dotted vertical line that descends to the left end of the baseline.

V.6) Occasionally an interjection or vocative will appear as the last word of a sentence. In that case, it may be connected either at the right end of the baseline or at the right end of the last word of the sentence, whichever location gives the strongest appearance of finality. The interjection or vocative would appear above and to the right of that final word, with a vertical dotted line connecting the left end of the interjection/vocative's slot to the right end of the final word's slot.

V.7) Noun clauses built on a stilt have the stilt connected to the verb slot of the noun clause's baseline. If the clause contains compound verbs, the stilt connects to the verb slot of the baseline, not one of the branches of the coordinating conjunction. A coordinate series of noun clauses introduced with a single conjunction or with no conjunction has the stilt connected to the left stub of the coordinating conjunction symbol that joins the clauses. The stilt connects at the left end of the stub, unless an introductory conjunction or interjection needs to connect there, in which case I lengthen the stub enough to allow space for the stilt to connect to the middle of the stub rather than on the endpoint. If the layout of the diagram can be improved by doing so, I connect the stilt to the end of the stub and the conjunction or interjection to the middle. In general, the first approach seems to work better with noun clauses above the baseline and the second with quotations placed below the baseline.

V.8) Where a noun clause or an infinitive phrase stands in apposition to a noun, the stilt for that clause or phrase rests on a horizontal line which is then connected to the head word with the appositive symbol (the equals sign).

V.9) When an appositive attaches to the subject of a clause, an introductory conjunction or interjection is diagrammed so that it, the left end of the subject line, and the right end of the appositive symbol form a three-way intersection.

V.10) Multiple modifiers to a single element are generally placed side-by-side, with the slot for that element elongated as much as necessary to allow this placement. In some diagrams more vertical than horizontal space is available, or there are simply too many modifiers or they are too long to arrange them side-by-side. In such cases the modifiers are placed in a vertical stack, with each successive modifier connected to the lower left corner of the one above it. A modifier connected to the lower left corner of another modifier is deemed to modify not the modifier to whose corner it connects but the first slot above it with which the connection point is *not* at the corner. Vertically stacked modifiers must have their upright connectors at the same angle. This does not mean that the angle of the connection for a particular kind of modifier can be varied; rather it limits the kind of modifiers that can be stacked. Differently angled (sets of) modifiers must connect to their head word's slot side-by-side. Of course extenders may be used as necessary (see section III.24.). Whenever possible, the order of occurrence within the text is preserved on the diagram, moving either left to right or top to bottom. The indirect object symbol presents a special problem in that it does not allow connection of another modifier at its lower left corner, with its leftward projection of the horizontal line. Therefore it must appear at the bottom of any vertical stack to which it belongs, regardless of its position in the text.

V.11) A conjunction introducing a compound sentence, especially a coordinating conjunction, is generally taken as introducing all the independent clauses, not just the first one. The introductory conjunction, then, connects to the left end of the stub of the coordinating conjunction symbol joining the clauses (unless the clauses share a single subject, in which case the conjunction connects, as usual, at the left end of the subject slot). Occasionally a subordinating conjunction seems to introduce only the first of a series of coordinate clauses. In that case, the conjunction symbol used to join the first clause to the others is a "zig-zag"-shaped symbol that consists of a dotted vertical coming down to the left end of a solid horizontal that takes the conjunction, with another dotted vertical descending from the right end of that horizontal. I found it necessary to use this symbol very few times, though its use would be defensible much more often.

VI. Policies governing the diagramming of ellipsis

Language in general is highly elliptical, and Greek is certainly no exception. A policy requiring the supply of every possible ellipsis would entail a great deal of additional diagramming and much guesswork about cases where more than one possibility, even with the same meaning, presents itself. Take, for example, just the question of the subjects of verbs. Since Greek verbs are inflected for person and number, the subject may often be omitted. A policy requiring every subject to be indicated explicitly might be helpful in many or most cases. But exactly what subject should be supplied? Should it simply be the appropriate personal pronoun, or should it be the noun to which that pronoun refers? What if a plural pronoun refers to a long coordinate series such as "the chief priests and scribes and Pharisees"? Must that whole series be supplied throughout a pericope for every verb of which they are the subject? This policy would not only require much tedious work but also introduce substantial space inefficiency. So it seems to me that anything gained by a policy requiring all ellipses to be supplied would be greatly outweighed by the difficulties introduced. The policy I follow is to supply ellipsis rather minimally, and generally with placeholders consisting of the capital letter X in parentheses rather than with explicit Greek words. Where the identity of the elliptical element is not easily inferred from the context and where there is little doubt about what it should be, I do supply Greek words in parentheses. Note that parentheses in the diagrams always indicate ellipsis; parentheses within the text itself are considered punctuation marks and are omitted from the diagrams (the square brackets, which are a text-critical indication rather than a discourse-flow indicator, are retained; cf. section II.3).

VI.1) Unexpressed subjects are always indicated by (X), the precise identification of the subject left to the reader.

VI.2) Unexpressed linking verbs are generally indicated by (X), though at times I do supply them.

VI.3) I also use ellipsis when necessary to construe a single modifier with more than one head. Wherever a diagram can be drawn so that the elements described by a particular modifier share a common point at which the modifier can be connected (which is always the stub of a coordinating conjunction symbol), I diagram the modifier once and connect it there. Where it is not possible to draw the diagram so, I diagram the modifier with the first item in the series and then supply it as an ellipsis with the others. This is different from the other uses of ellipsis described above; in those cases words necessary for complete grammatical expression are actually unexpressed in the text. In this situation the grammar is complete; I use the ellipsis only to indicate that the words I am placing in the diagram at a particular point do not actually occur in the Greek text. The potential point of confusion is the fact that they actually do occur in the text; they just do not occur in the text separately for each time they appear in the diagram.

VI.4) Clauses introduced by ὡς and lacking a verb are discussed at length in section VII.9.

VII. Policies governing the diagramming of specific grammatical constructions

VII.1) Substantive adjectives are treated like nouns, as opposed to being diagrammed as modifiers for an elliptical head word.

VII.2) It is not always easy to decide whether to construe nouns in the oblique cases as direct objects or adverbs. The guiding principle is whether verb is transitive, that is, whether its action is of such a nature that it can be performed upon an object rather than being self-contained. The question is often clouded by the nature of the English verbs most commonly used to translate the Greek verb. For example, is διακονέω transitive ("serve," an action that takes an object) or intransitive ("minister," which is self-contained)? Does the dative case after διακονέω name the one who is served or the one in whose interests someone ministers? This is not an easy question to answer, at least not for me. My policy has been to ask first whether the verb is transitive or intransitive. Often BDAG specifically tags verbs as transitive or intransitive, which is of course very helpful, and I generally follow their guidance. But when the matter is murky, if the direct object seems reasonably defensible, then I diagram a direct object. So in the case of διακονέω I diagram the dative as the object. Verbs with prepositional prefixes introduce the additional issue of whether the noun relates most closely to the verb stem or to the preposition. Where the noun seems to provide the object of the prepositional prefix (though not necessarily in the case normally governed by that preposition) but not the verb stem, I consider the noun adverbial.

VII.3) A parenthetical clause may be diagrammed as a subordinate clause with "(paren)" supplied as the conjunction on the subordinate clause symbol.

VII.4) An article accompanying an infinitive is never diagrammed in the infinitive slot, since that slot is a verb slot and in no way can an article be considered as belonging to a phrasal verb. The article with any infinitive used substantivally goes into the noun slot (often the subject or direct object slot), and the infinitive is raised on a stilt resting in that same slot, positioned after the article.

VII.5) One specific construction involving the articular infinitive is the infinitive used in a prepositional phrase. Since the infinitive is a verbal noun, it can readily function as the object of a preposition. The infinitive in a prepositional phrase, therefore, is constructed with a right-angle prepositional phrase symbol containing the preposition and the infinitive's article in the preposition and object slots respectively. The infinitive itself is raised on a stilt, and any subject, complement, or modifiers are then attached to that baseline as usual. In the relatively rare construction with πρὶν ἤ, the two-word phrase is treated as the preposition. An alternative would be to diagram πρίν as an adverb, then attach beneath it an adverbial infinitive with ἤ attached to the upright as a subordinating conjunction.

VII.6) Another common construction with the articular infinitive uses the genitive article. This construction has a variety of usages, the adverbial function being most common and the explanatory function appearing often enough to deserve mention. In keeping with the pattern described above, the article is diagrammed on the symbol appropriate to the construction (a right-angle adverb being most common), with the infinitive raised on a stilt resting to the right of the article. On strict grammatical principles, one would expect this construction to indicate that the infinitive is in the genitive case. Most instances may indeed be interpreted so, but in a few cases, especially in Luke's writings, it seems that the construction must be understood as a subject phrase even though it is in the genitive case. Luke 17:1 is an example; if τοῦ τὰ σκάνδαλα μὴ ἐλθεῖν is not the subject, then ἐστιν is left with no subject at all. If one is willing to accept such a construction as valid, then the genitive infinitive phrase could perhaps be construed as explanatory to ἀνένδεκτον in this verse. But in Acts 10:25 there is no suitable word for the infinitive to explain, and the subject use seems the only one possible. So it seems as though the genitive article with the infinitive has come to be used sometimes as a marker of a substantival use of the infinitive without necessarily specifying its case.

VII.7) Indirect discourse participles are sometimes difficult to distinguish from the object/complement construction. This topic is discussed in section III.20. and under εὑρίσκω in section IX.

VII.8) Relative pronouns have a dual nature that presents a diagramming challenge. These pronouns agree with their antecedent in gender and number and often in case. Because a relative pronoun generally introduces a clause that modifies the antecedent, the natural instinct is to diagram the pronoun as attributive to its antecedent. However, the relative pronoun also has a noun function within its clause, and it is impossible to diagram a single word as simultaneously, for example, attributive to a noun in one clause and direct object of a verb in another. The solution to this dilemma is to diagram the relative pronoun showing its grammatical function within the clause it introduces, not in relation to the antecedent, and then show the attributive relationship of the whole relative clause to its head word by connecting the relative pronoun back to its antecedent with a dotted line or curve. The relative clause, then, floats unconnected to the rest of the sentence except for that dotted line or curve. Sometimes the antecedent is not expressed, in which case the slot where an explicit antecedent would appear will be filled with (X). Occasionally a prepositional phrase with a relative pronoun functions in place of a conjunction, e.g. Rom. 5:12. In these cases, because I cannot find any antecedent for the pronoun at all, either explicit or implicit, I diagram the prepositional phrase as a phrasal conjunction. Although I am not at all certain that this approach is entirely true to Greek idiom, no superior approach has yet occurred to me. Another thorny construction involving the relative pronoun is that in which the pronoun precedes its antecedent and seems to modify it, such as the English phrase "in which case," which appears earlier in this paragraph. As best I can determine, the pronoun's antecedent is the whole idea of the preceding clause, although the pronoun is written in the gender and number of the noun it seems to modify (e.g. δι' ἣν αἰτίαν in 2Ti. 1:6,12; Tit. 1:13, and Heb. 2:11). Uncertain again about which approach is really truest to the nature of the Greek, I diagram these constructions with the relative pronoun as the object of the preposition, followed by the noun set in apposition to the pronoun. Where possipossible, I then connect the pronoun back to the verb of the clause to which it seems to refer. The reason I diagram in this way rather than letting the noun be the object of the preposition, modified by the relative pronoun, is that it seems to me that the core of the phrase includes the relative pronoun and that the noun is added for clarification. This makes the pronoun the head word and the noun its expansion. I am open to suggestions for improvement on these difficult constructions involving the relative pronoun.

VII.9) Constructions where ὡς introduces a verbless phrase present special issues. "Be wise as serpents and harmless as doves" is straightforward: the full expression is "Be wise as serpents (are wise) and harmless as doves (are harmless)." The only diagramming decision to be made is whether to supply the predicate along with the elliptical linking verbs (in the interest of compactness, I do not). But the first part of the same verse (Mat. 10:16) is more problematic: "I send you as sheep among wolves" could be expanded "I send you as (I would send) sheep among wolves" (πρόβατα accusative, direct object) or "I send you as (though you were) sheep among wolves" (πρόβατα predicate nominative) which could be condensed with an accusative participle to "I send you as (being) sheep among wolves" (πρόβατα predicate accusative). Parallel constructions involving masculine or feminine nouns (where the case of the noun is unambiguous) pretty well eliminate the second option by regularly using the accusative case (e.g. Mat. 3:16). In general, I construe a nominative after ὡς as the subject of the elliptical verb and the other cases as complements after elliptical participles of εἰμί.

VII.10) Hanging (pendent) constructions—usually but not always in the nominative. The hanging element is diagrammed on a horizontal line which is then connected with the resumptive element in the main clause with a vertical dotted line (even if the pendent element is in another case). An example of such a construction in English would be, "That boy, I saw him in the park yesterday." *Boy* would be diagrammed on a horizontal line, above the baseline, with the vertical dotted line joining it to *him* in the direct object slot of the baseline.

VII.11) The preposition εἰς is sometimes used reflecting the Semitic idiom where ל introduces the predicate after a linking verb. I diagram these constructions with the εἰς phrase on an inline prepositional phrase symbol connected to the end of the baseline after the linking verb and slanted predicate divider. A good alternative (actually better in some ways, I would say) would be to raise the prepositional phrase on a stilt resting in the predicate noun/adjective slot. The main reason behind my policy for this construction is simply to make it stand out as unusual. To the objection that the vertical divider within the prepositional phrase might be mistaken as indicating the direct object of the verb, I would reply that the linking verb and the slanted predicate divider prevent this misunderstanding well enough.

VII.12) Noun clauses are most commonly introduced by the conjunctions ὅτι and ἵνα. Occasionally, however, other words such as εἰ, ὡς and πῶς may function in this way and are diagrammed accordingly.

VII.13) A common Semitic construction that seems clearly to have found its way into Biblical Greek is a head noun followed by two genitives, the first of which expresses something like a quality and the second of which is a personal pronoun. An example is Col. 1:13, εἰς τὴν βασιλείαν τοῦ υἱοῦ τῆς ἀγάπης αὐτοῦ, where the meaning is clearly "the kingdom of his beloved son" rather than "the kingdom of the son of his love." I am quite ready to see this construction in passages where it is debatable, such as Luke 1:44, ἡ φωνὴ τοῦ ἀσπασμοῦ σου and Luke 1:51, διανοίᾳ καρδίας αὐτῶν. I diagram these passages to reflect the meaning that I consider most likely, often with a passage note to acknowledge the alternative.

VII.14) The cognate accusative is diagrammed as either a direct object or an adverb, depending on its relationship to the action of the verb. In Mat. 6:19 (μὴ θησαυρίζετε ὑμῖν θησαυρούς) it is direct object; in Luke 2:9 (ἐφοβήθησαν φόβον μέγαν) it is adverbial.

VII.15) It is my understanding that first- and second-person verbs as well as third-person verbs may have explicit subjects in the nominative case. Thus in Eph. 4:13 (μέχρι καταντήσωμεν οἱ πάντες), I diagram οἱ πάντες as the subject. It seems to me that the view that only third-person verbs can have explicit subjects is a matter of English grammar and not Greek.

VII.16) I diagram the periphrastic construction with the linking verb and the participle together as a phrasal verb in the verb slot. I always put the linking verb first, regardless of the order of the elements in the sentence.

VII.17) Modifiers to the noun concept of a substantive participle are diagrammed beneath the noun slot on which the substantive stilt rests. Modifiers to the verb concept of a substantive participle are diagrammed beneath the participle itself. The article of a substantive participle is placed on the substantive participle symbol right along with the participle. (This differs from the practice with articular infinitives, where the article goes in the noun slot rather than on the line with the infinitive. The basis for the difference is the fact that the double vertical line on the infinitive symbol identifies the infinitive's slot as a verb slot, and an article has no place there. An accusative of general reference could be connected to the left of the infinitive, and the article would look exceedingly strange in the verb slot of a baseline. No such issue arises with the substantive participle, so I diagram the article and the participle together.)

VII.18) Sometimes an "extra" article is written along with a genitive noun, indicating a substantival or attributive function of that noun. Gal. 5:24 (οἱ τοῦ Χριστοῦ) is an example of the former; Gal. 2:20 (πίστει...τῇ τοῦ υἱοῦ τοῦ θεοῦ) of the latter. For the attributive construction, I place the extra article right along with the genitive noun on a single adjective symbol. For the substantival construction, though, the article is pronominal and the genitive noun has a genitive-case relationship to it. So I diagram the article in the appropriate noun slot and the genitive as an adjectival modifier to it.

VII.19) Sometimes it is difficult to decide which of two nominatives (or, where the verb is an infinitive, which of two accusatives) is the subject and which is the predicate. Of course there are patterns of article usage that often decide the case. But where the placement of any articles leaves the question open, I am generally able to resolve the matter (to my own satisfaction, at least) by asking which of the two nominatives refers to the topic under discussion and which presents the new information in the form of a statement or question about that topic. The former, of course, is then construed as subject and the latter as predicate. Wallace's grammar outlines additional grammatical considerations that generally lead to the same conclusion. Where the two approaches clearly lead to different conclusions, the approach reflecting the definitions of subject and predicate seems to me to carry more weight than Wallace's approach that discriminates on the basis of parts of speech and grammatical mechanics. Where the definitional approach does not seem to yield a clear conclusion, though, one does well to apply Wallace's scheme.

VII.20) Predicate nouns and adjectives most commonly complete the linking verbs εἰμί, γίνομαι, and ὑπάρχω. However, many other verbs can be construed with predicate adjectives or predicate nouns. Any word in the predicate of a sentence that agrees with the subject in case could potentially be construed as predicate noun or adjective. The question is whether its main function is to rename or describe the subject, providing a key component of the clause's assertion or question about the subject. Thus in Rev. 16:15 (ἵνα μὴ γυμνὸς περιπατῇ, "lest he should walk naked"), γυμνός is best construed as predicate adjective. One way to discern these more unusual uses of the predicate noun or adjective is to replace the clause's verb with a linking verb. If the sense of the sentence does not greatly change and the noun or adjective in question would supply the complement for the linking verb, then almost certainly the predicate noun or adjective use is best.

VII.21) Sometimes it is difficult to decide which of two adjectival words functions as the substantive and which as the attributive. The method by which I answer such questions is to ask this: can I discern that one of the words would better stand alone as the key idea with the other providing a more incidental description? The word whose omission would least damage the thought of the passage is the attributive; the more necessary word is the substantive.

VII.22) A construction found in many languages but whose frequency in the NT may reflect some Semitic influence via the Septuagint is the statement of possession in the form "X is to Y," using a linking verb with Y in the dative case to convey the idea that "Y has X." Thus in Luke 1:7, οὐκ ἦν αὐτοῖς τέκνον means "They did not have a child." I diagram this construction with the dative case on an adverb symbol modifying the linking verb. Incidentally, English also uses this construction where what is "possessed" is a quality: "There is a striking beauty to that picture" means "That picture has a striking beauty."

VII.23) Passive verbs can take objects. A verb whose active voice can take a double accusative construction, when shifted to the passive, is generally written with the person as the subject and the thing as a retained object. The idea is that the verb even in the passive voice continues to have two recipients of its action: one is the subject and the other is this retained object. A retained object is diagrammed on a direct object symbol, like an ordinary direct object. In my opinion a passive verb may also have an indirect object. If the nature of the verb's action would justify an indirect object in an active-voice construction, nothing about its use in the passive voice changes the appropriateness of the indirect object.

VII.24) The emphatic double negative οὐ μή is diagrammed as an adverbial unit.

VII.25) There is a Semitic construction expressing the partitive idea with a simple prepositional phrase using ἐκ or ἀπό (e.g., Mat. 23:34 ἐξ αὐτῶν ἀποκτενεῖτε, "[Some] of them you will kill"). One could justifiably diagram this construction with the substantival prepositional phrase symbol, but I opted to supply an elliptical head word for the prepositional phrase to modify.

VII.26) There is a Semitic construction expressing an oath using the conditional particle "if." For example, in Mark 8:12, Jesus says, ἀμὴν λέγω ὑμῖν, εἰ δοθήσεται τῇ γενεᾷ ταύτῃ σημεῖον ("Truly I say to you, no sign will be given to this generation"). The meaning is something like, "Truly I say to you, [God is not God] if a sign will be given to this generation." I diagram this construction by supplying an elliptical main clause with no subject or verb expressed, so that the clause introduced by εἰ can be diagrammed as subordinate.

VIII. Policies governing the diagramming of various kinds of coordination

The symbols used to diagram coordination present the need for some special considerations. There are four such symbols, which I will distinguish based on the location of the stub that connects it to the slot whose contents the conjunction divides into a series: one with the connecting stub on the left end of the symbol, on with it on the right, one with it on both ends, and one with no stub at all. I will refer to these respectively as "left-stub series," "right-stub series," "double-stub series," and "no-stub series."

VIII.1) The left-stub series is by far the most frequently used.

VIII.2) The right-stub series is used primarily where a series of subjects shares a single verb and there is no introductory conjunction or interjection.

VIII.3) I use the no-stub series for coordination where a left-stub series is needed but there is nothing further left in the diagram to which to connect it. For example, a sentence having two or more independent clauses and lacking an introductory conjunction or interjection uses the no-stub series.

VIII.4) Some situations require a double-stub series. For example, a sentence may contain a pair of subject/verb combinations that share a single object and a single introductory conjunction.

VIII.5) Sometimes a pair of conjunctions or other words combines to express coordination. Examples include but are not limited to "both...and," "either...or" and "neither...nor." I show that these words work together by stacking them vertically in the conjunction area along the dotted line of the coordinating conjunction symbol. I use this approach for variations on "not...but" as well, even though the negative is not a conjunction and doing so loses the connection between "not" and the specific word within its clause that it negates. For "not only...but also" I diagram all four words in two pairs: "not only" on top and "but also" on the bottom. Two constructions come to mind where I do *not* stack the conjunctions like some others do. One is "(just) as...so (also)," and the other is "if...then." The reason I do not treat these as coordinate is that it seems clear to me that there is actually a subordinate relationship of one to the other in each case, the "just as" and "if" clauses being the subordinate ones. The "if...then" combination does not appear so often in the Greek NT, which generally omits the conjunction introducing the apodosis (the "then" clause).

VIII.6) At times a clause that coordinates with another on the grammatical level has a subordinate relationship on the logical level. So, for example, Jesus tells the prospective disciples, "Follow me, and I will make you fishers of men." Even grammatically speaking, the coordination is only partial, since the first verb is imperative and the second is indicative. At some level of the exegetical process, the interpreter must wrestle with the exact nature of the coordination in each case: is the series truly coordinate, or is there some underlying logical development? In this case it is easy to see that the second clause expresses the outcome of the first. But sentence diagramming is one of the initial stages of the exegetical process, and the aim is to account for the grammatical relationships, not necessarily the semantic or logical relationships. So where coordinating conjunctions are used, I diagram coordinate relationships, leaving further refinement to later stages of the exegetical process.

VIII.7) Many passages contain coordinate series of three or more items, and in many cases a clear pattern of what we might call subcoordination may be discerned. So, for example, a coordinate series of four items might consist of two pairs of items that cohere with one another more closely than they cohere with the items in the other pair. An example I like to use is, "For supper we had steak and potatoes and cake and ice cream." Where such subdivision within a longer series is evident, I generally reflect it by using more than one coordinating conjunction symbol. The example above would use three left-stub series symbols: steak and potatoes would be paired on one, cake and ice cream on one, and the third would pair the two pairs and connect the whole series to the direct object slot of the baseline. A good NT example of subsetted coordination is Luke 2:9, where the first two clauses describe events external to the shepherds and the third states their response. Where such subdivision cannot be made out clearly, or where there seems to be more than one equally valid way to subdivide, I generally diagram a single longer series, although I suppose I tend to err on the side of diagramming the subcoordination that I see most clearly, even if the scheme is perhaps debatable.

VIII.8) The conjunction καί, when followed by a few words that begin with ε, joins itself to the following word much like some pairs of English words contract. The most common of these is κἀγώ, which is the crasis (the Greek term for contraction) of καί and ἐγώ. In these cases the two words must be split apart so that καί can be diagrammed separately from the other word.

VIII.9) Another situation in which I divide words, although this one is not a case of necessity, is where a negative that could be shown as part of a dual conjunction is separated from the rest of the word in order to be diagrammed so. An example would be the word οὐκέτι (Mark 10:8). Astute readers of the diagrams may notice that I did not do this consistently (cf. 1Ti. 5:23); I confess this weakness but doubt that I will have occasion to make corrections.

VIII.10) An apparently Semitic construction appears with some frequency, in which an initial coordinating conjunction introduces a clause (often with ἐγένετο in the sense, "and it happened"), and then a redundant καί appears before the clause expressing the main action of the sentence. How I diagram the conjunctions depends on the nature of the overall construction. Where the main action of the sentence is a noun clause functioning as subject of ἐγένετο, I diagram the initial conjunction as usual, connected to the left end of the baseline for ἐγένετο. I then diagram the redundant καί as an introductory conjunction on the left end of the subject clause baseline. Some instances of this construction are Mat. 9:10 and Luke 5:1,12,17. Where the sentence's main clause is not a noun clause, I do not have two different baselines to work with. So I diagram the redundant conjunctions side-by-side, on separate introductory conjunction symbols, with the first at the left end of the baseline and the second just to the right of the first. An example is Luke 7:12.

VIII.11) Sometimes a coordinate series of modifiers contains items that would call for the connectors at different angles (e.g., "the true and living God" contains an adjective and a participle modifying *God*). I follow a "pecking order" in which verbs get precedence over verbals, which in turn get precedence over other words. So in the example mentioned, the participle would take precedence over the adjective and the connecting segment would be vertical. However, if there are three or more items in the series, I allow a majority of lower-precedence items to override a minority of higher-precedence items.

IX. **Policies governing the diagramming of constructions involving specific words or phrases, listed in alphabetical order**

ἀνά. A passage note on the diagram for Mat. 20:9-10 discusses at some length the diagramming of the distributive use of this preposition.

ἐὰν μή. I often diagram this expression as a single conjunction unit.

ἐγγύς. BDAG categorizes the word as either an adverb or a preposition with genitive object. When used with a genitive, I diagram it as a preposition with the genitive as its object. Some may prefer to construe ἐγγύς as an adverb modified by the genitive.

εἰ. See section VII.26 for the Semitic construction where this conjunction introduces an oath.

εἰ δὲ μὴ γέ. This conglomeration of particles is bit of a challenge to unpack, though it turns out that each word is able to carry pretty much its normal function. δέ coordinates the clause introduced by this phrase with something in the preceding context. εἰ can be construed as introducing an elliptical subordinate clause (conditional). μή modifies the verb of the elliptical clause, and the least objectionable way to treat γέ seems to me take it as intensifying μή.

εἰ μή. I often diagram this expression as a single conjunction unit.

ἐπαισχύνομαι. I construe the accusative as adverbial, not direct object.

εὑρίσκω. The verb is often completed by a substantive and a participle. It is difficult to decide whether to take the construction as indirect discourse or as object/complement. I distinguish the two on the following basis: if the participle expresses an action, I diagram indirect discourse. If it expresses a state, I diagram object/complement. An example of the former is Mat. 20:6 εὗρεν ἄλλους ἑστῶτας; of the latter, Luke 7:10 εὗρον τὸν δοῦλον ὑγιαίνοντα. A few examples remain ambiguous; for example Mat. 26:40 εὑρίσκει αὐτοὺς καθεύδοντας. Is "sleeping" an action or a state? I opted for action and diagrammed indirect discourse. See also section III.20.

ζημιόω. BDAG appears to interpret the accusative case as accusative of reference rather than direct object.

Ἰησοῦς Χριστός, Χριστὸς Ἰησοῦς. I diagram the expression as a single noun unit rather than splitting it apart into two nouns in apposition. This is not because I do not think apposition is inappropriate but is rather for the sake of saving space. I did not feel that the appositional connection within this very common designation for our Lord was important enough to warrant the space inefficiency that would be required always to show it. Where κύριος is included, however, I did diagram apposition between that noun and this expression.

ἵνα μή. I often diagram this expression as a single conjunction unit.

καλέω. In the passive the verb often takes a predicate noun or adjective; in the active it sometimes takes an object/complement construction (e.g. Mat. 1:21 καλέσεις τὸ ὄνομα αὐτοῦ Ἰησοῦν).

μή. See sections III.3 and VII.24. Also, this negative may be diagrammed as a conjunction introducing a subordinate clause (expressing a negative purpose) or even a noun clause in some contexts.

μηδείς. See the entry for οὐδείς below.

ὅ τι. This expression is several times to be understood as the neuter indefinite relative from ὅστις (e.g., Mark 6:23, ὅ τι ἐάν με αἰτήσῃς δώσω σοι). It is written as two words in some editions (including NA28) to avoid confusion with the conjunction ὅτι. I diagram it as though it were a single word, since it is no different in function from the other forms of ὅστις, which are always written as single words. Occasionally it may even be taken as interrogative, equivalent to τί (e.g., Mark 9:11, 28; see BDAG, ὅστις, 4.b.).

οὐ. See sections III.3 and VII.24.

οὐδείς. When used with a noun or another expression that could be construed as substantival, I generally construe οὐδείς as adjectival to the other term. It seems to me that that other term carries the key idea while this word specifies a quantity of zero. This is the opposite form of the same principle underlying the comments on πᾶς below.

πᾶς. With adjectival words, I almost always, if not always, diagram the other word as carrying the noun function and πᾶς as adjectival. The thinking is that the other word carries the key idea and is therefore the head word, while πᾶς is subsidiary, specifying a universal quantity of that idea. This is the opposite form of the same principle underlying the comments on οὐδείς above. Another question worthy of comment is whether πᾶς can take a genitive of the whole. Many phrases seem to be open to that understanding, etc. πάντων ὑμῶν. Careful inquiry, though, will discover that nominative, dative, or accusative πᾶς is never followed by a genitive of the whole. Rather, the word that *might* have been a genitive of the whole after a substantive πᾶς rather agrees with πᾶς in case (e.g., πάντας ὑμᾶς). This means that the other word, not πᾶς, is carrying the function of the head noun, and πᾶς is its attributive modifier therefore agreeing in gender, number and case. So, no, πᾶς does not take a genitive of the whole and must therefore be diagrammed, when used in phrases like this in the genitive, as modifying that other word, not as modified by it. This makes it unlike indefinite τις, which often has a genitive of the whole attached. To any who object to this inconsistency ("Why should *some* take the partitive construction while *all* does not?), I would say, simply, "Welcome to the world of language, where all is not always neat and tidy!" The usage pattern is clear and consistent, regardless of what we might wish the Greeks hand done in developing their language. English is no better. Earlier in this document I used the phrases "on top" and "on the bottom" in direct contrast. Why isn't English consistent in its use of the article in this pair of expressions? If we can omit the article from "on the top," why can't we omit it from "on the bottom"? Like it or not, anything approaching perfect consistency simply is not a property of human language, and the grammarian is obligated to reckon with what *is*, not to try to make things be what he or she thinks they *should* be. End of grammatical sermon!

ποιέω. The word sometimes appears with a complement consisting of a noun and an infinitive. Luke 5:34 is a good example: μὴ δύνασθε τοὺς υἱοὺς τοῦ νυμφῶνος...ποιῆσαι νηστεῦσαι; ("You cannot make the sons of the bridal chamber to fast, can you?"). When one asks "make what?" in order to identify the complement, it is clear that υἱούς is not the object of the verb. So the clause cannot be diagrammed with υἱούς as object. The complement is the whole idea that the sons of the bridal chamber fast. So the construction is indirect discourse; this takes υἱούς out of the direct object slot and places it into the accusative of general reference slot, consistently with its function as specifying the one who does the fasting. So, even though "discourse" in no sense describes the nature of the action of ποιέω, the construction does accurately reflect the grammatical relationships among the various words. Of course there are other complementary constructions with this verb, but the others are much more straightforward and do not require comment here.

πρῶτος. The adjective often agrees with a substantive and yet seems clearly to function adverbially (e.g. 1Ti. 2:13 Ἀδὰμ γὰρ πρῶτος ἐπλάσθη). I diagram it as an adverb in such cases.

τίς (interrogative). This word sometimes functions as a relative pronoun and therefore I diagram it as such where appropriate. See BDAG, τίς, 1.a.β.ℸ.

τολμάω. I diagram the infinitive after this word in the direct object slot as its complement.

Χριστὸς Ἰησοῦς, Ἰησοῦς Χριστός. See Ἰησοῦς Χριστός above.

ὡς. Policies for diagramming verbless clauses introduced by ὡς are discussed at length above, section VII.9. Sometimes ὡς is used along with a word expressing quantity to convey an idea of approximation; such uses may be diagrammed as simple modifiers to the word expressing quantity. Occasionally the word is used with an ordinary noun to express a similar idea of approximation. For example, in Rev. 19:1 John writes ἤκουσα ὡς φωνὴν μεγάλην ὄχλου. Without ὡς the statement would be straightforward: "I heard the sound of a great crowd"; ὡς adds the idea of approximation that we would express in English using "something like": "I heard something like the sound of a great crowd." This construction could perhaps be diagrammed with an elliptical object modified somehow by the ὡς phrase, but I opted simply to put ὡς right along with the noun in the noun's own slot (in this example the direct object slot). It seems to me that the presence of ὡς does not change the essential function of the noun. BDAG seems to be of the same mind; see ὡς, 2.c. A third alternative, which may perhaps be better yet and which I may adopt at some future time is to mirror the construction where ὡς modifies a quantity: simply diagram it as adjectival to the noun.

www.ingramcontent.com/pod-product-compliance
Lightning Source LLC
Chambersburg PA
CBHW050454110426
42743CB00017B/3363